Happy Anniversary!

Robin A. Kring

Meadowbrook Press

Distributed by Simon & Schuster
New York

Library of Congress Cataloging-in-Publication Data
Kring, Robin.
    Happy anniversary! / Robin A. Kring.
        p. cm.
    ISBN 0-88166-361-1(Meadowbrook)—ISBN 0-671-31815-2 (Simon &
Schuster)
    1. Wedding anniversaries—Planning. 2. Entertaining. I. Title.
GT2800 .K75 2000
793.2—dc21   99-058720
                                                              CIP

Managing Editor: Christine Zuchora-Walske
Copyeditors: Joseph Gredler, Kathleen Martin-James
Proofreader: Megan McGinnis
Production Manager: Joe Gagne
Desktop Publishing: Danielle White
Illustrations: Terri Moll

Published by Meadowbrook Press, 5451 Smetana Drive, Minnetonka,
Minnesota 55343

www.meadowbrookpress.com

BOOK TRADE DISTRIBUTION by Simon & Schuster, a division of
Simon and Schuster, Inc., 1230 Avenue of the Americas, New York,
New York 10020

04 03 02 01 00   10 9 8 7 6 5 4 3 2 1

Printed in the United States of America

Dedication

To my brother, Robert, and his wife, Tamala,
a lifetime of "Happy Anniversary!" wishes

Acknowledgments

This book owes its existence to Bruce Lansky, who conceived the idea for *Happy Anniversary!* Thank you for the opportunity to write this book. I started this project with my editor, Liya Lev Oertel, whose expertise and encouragement have greatly benefited my writing. A sincere thank-you to my new managing editor, Christine Zuchora-Walske, and copyeditors, Joseph Gredler and Kathleen Martin-James, for polishing my work to a glossy shine.

A special thank-you to the many party hosts and event professionals who have shared their creative ideas, especially Sue Beggs, Adele Emerson, Melody Page, Joyce and Evis Robinson, Marsha Slack, and Karen Wendell.

In memory of my mom, I express my gratitude for her introduction to the joy, fun, and enchantment of party making. And, to Dad, thank you for your thoughtful, wise, and—yes—humorous spirit that influences my writing and very being. A special thank-you for the twenty dollars you gave me to get by between book advances. (Just kidding!)

Finally, I thank my soul mate, Michael, for his unwavering support, burning of the midnight oil, and dreaming of our own lifetime of anniversary parties.

Contents

The Ninth Anniversary: Pottery and Willow

The Tenth Anniversary: Tin

The Eleventh Anniversary: Steel

The Twelfth Anniversary: Silk

The Thirteenth Anniversary: Lace

The Fourteenth Anniversary: Ivory

The Fifteenth Anniversary: Crystal

The Sixteenth through Nineteenth Anniversaries:
Sweet Imaginations

The Twentieth Anniversary: China

The Twenty-Fifth Anniversary: Silver

The Thirtieth Anniversary: Pearl

The Thirty-Fifth Anniversary: Coral

The Fortieth Anniversary: Ruby

The Forty-Fifth Anniversary: Sapphire

The Fiftieth Anniversary: Gold

The Fifty-Fifth Anniversary: Emerald

The Sixtieth Anniversary and Beyond: Diamond

Appendices

Introduction

The History of Wedding Anniversary Traditions

The custom of celebrating what was once referred to as the "anniversary wedding" can be traced back to the Victorian era. Genteel Victorians wrote detailed deportment guides for entertaining, dress, and conduct. These guides described the proper etiquette for anniversary weddings right along with the art of conversation and the correct placement of silver. At that time, an important element of any proper anniversary wedding was bestowing symbolic gifts upon the anniversary couple.

Although no one is certain how the traditional list of symbolic anniversary gifts originated, it is likely that the Victorians made the custom popular. They loved to use gifts and personal ornaments to convey meaning. Victorians often presented tussie-mussies, small bouquets gathered with bits of lace and ribbon, to communicate private messages. Each flower symbolized a different sentiment. Daisies, for example, represented innocence, while pansies represented thoughtful recollection. Many young women also used "fan talk"—a secret code for communicating devotion to their suitors. For example, if a woman hid her face behind an open fan, this meant "I love you." If she lowered the fan over her chest, she implored, "Wait for me." Even wedding bands carried special messages. Some brides spelled their grooms' names in gemstones. Robert, for example, might have been spelled **r**uby, **o**pal, **b**loodstone, **e**merald, **r**uby, **t**opaz.

Early anniversary symbolism included only a few of the anniversaries we recognize today. Emily Post listed "eight anniversaries known to all" in her 1922 *Blue Book of Social Usage*:

> One year: paper
> Five years: wood
> Ten years: tin
> Fifteen years: crystal
> Twenty years: china
> Twenty-five years: silver
> Fifty years: gold
> Seventy-five years: diamond

Mrs. Post then went on to report that "until comparatively modern times, the eight anniversaries were all that were acknowledged." She then recognized the trend toward celebrating additional anniversaries and listed a symbolic anniversary gift for each of the first fifteen years of marriage and one for every five years after that. This is the basis for the lists we use today.

Victorian etiquette books not only described symbolic anniversary gifts and coordinating party decorations but also gave extensive anniversary-planning advice that might sound rather amusing today. In the 1882 book *Our Deportment or the Manners, Conduct and Dress of the Most Refined Society*, John H. Young, A.M. suggested that "at earlier anniversaries much pleasantry and amusement is occasioned by presenting unique and fantastic articles . . . [although] care should be taken that they should not be such as are liable to give offense to a person of sensitive nature."

Anniversary symbolism and gift ideas continued to be recorded over the years. As some gifts became outdated due to developing technology and mass production, new suggestions replaced them. For instance, aluminum replaced tin as the traditional tenth anniversary designation. Today, it's hard to imagine why a couple would want either tin or aluminum gifts. Several other gift designations also seem archaic or valueless. An old iron skillet is no longer considered a treasured gift passed down from generation to generation.

Gradually, modern choices were added to the list alongside the traditional choices. Diamond jewelry was added as the modern tenth anniversary designation, and clocks were listed as the first anniversary choice. Gift suggestions and the years designated continue to vary from author to author and country to country. For instance, some German lists register tin not on the tenth anniversary as American lists do but on the six-and-one-half year wedding anniversary.

Currently, Hallmark Cards, Inc. publishes the most popular gift list, which is traditionally printed in its complimentary pocket calendar. One can follow such an anniversary symbol list (see Appendix A) in anniversary gift giving and party planning. I have also included several contemporary twists on traditional gift suggestions in each chapter of this book.

The custom of anniversary weddings has evolved into our present day celebration of wedding anniversaries. The most common—or as many etiquette books have put it, the most important—are the twenty fifth (silver) anniversary and the fiftieth (golden) anniversary. However, every anniversary is an important milestone in a couple's married life. With divorce so common today, keeping a loving and considerate marriage together is a success to celebrate. Every anniversary should commemorate a flourishing relationship that has enriched both partners. So revel in the charming anniversary year traditions with creative flair. Don't wait until the popular twenty-five and fifty-year celebrations to throw a party. Celebrate along the way with anniversary fun and festivity!

Observe each wedding anniversary with a commemorative gift, a special moment for two, or an imaginative party. The following celebrations are inspired by a traditional sparkle and enchanted with unique expression. These romantic celebrations are truly each an anniversary creation!

Planning an Anniversary to Remember

Anniversaries, particularly the milestone twenty-fifth, fortieth, fiftieth, and sixtieth, are significant lifetime occasions—each deserving a unique expression of romance. Planning an anniversary to remember is easy with this book's creative, at-your-fingertips designs. Feel free to adapt each celebration to the anniversary couple. Does the fifth anniversary couple love movies? If so, there's no need to wait until the tenth anniversary for a Tinsel Town anniversary party. Take thematic license and adapt this celebration for a five-year anniversary. The same goes for individual ideas listed in other themes. Perhaps you're planning an eight-year anniversary and like the first anniversary's "Paper Picnic Poetics" suggestion for reminiscing over wedding photos and scrapbooks. You also like the idea of laying a string trail to anniversary gifts as mentioned in the "Wool 'n' Copper Capers" seventh anniversary party design. Use them both. Listed ideas aren't exclusive to any one design. You can also bend the rules a little and throw an anniversary party a few years off the actual milestone date. For example, maybe you'll find the twenty-second anniversary year more appropriate than the twentieth year to throw a "China and Champagne Supper."

When planning anniversary parties, also consider the special needs of the anniversary couple and guests. Perhaps an anniversary husband's or wife's health limits his or her activity. Scale the celebration accordingly by hosting a quiet yet festive home celebration. Plan the time and menu according to the anniversary couple's preferences. There's a lot of flexibility within these anniversary creations. The design ideas can be implemented as simply or extravagantly as desired. Apply a few ideas to accent an intimate gathering or plan an extravagant anniversary gala.

Hosting the Anniversary Party

Who hosts the anniversary? The answer isn't etched in formal etiquette stone. It's quite appropriate for a close friend, family member, or even the anniversary couple to throw a party in celebration of the wedding anniversary. Politeness and good taste, though, do dictate that the most formal occasions, such as a silver jubilee, golden wedding gala, or diamond cotillion, be hosted by a family member. Although these and other anniversaries may be officially hosted by a family member or close friend, the anniversary couple can be very involved in their planning and design.

The Invitation

The invitation sets the stage for the event and provides an opportunity to make a spectacular first impression. I like to use eye-popping invitations that capture guests' attention immediately. It's not likely that guests will forget a unique Cracker Jack box inviting them to a "Big Top Anniversary Circus" or an engraved faux-silver tray requesting the pleasure of their company at a "Silver Wedding Jubilee." Make a dramatic statement by wrapping an invitation with a beautiful organdy or satin ribbon or by delivering an invitation with a bouquet of roses or colorful balloons. A sensational invitation adds to the excitement surrounding an event because it hints at a party bursting with enthusiastic expression. (Hint: Pack the invitation carefully in a mailing box or bubble-wrap envelope and check with the U.S. Postal Service to ensure proper postage.)

The anniversary party marks the celebration of a period of time. Therefore, when designing invitations, include the wedding and anniversary years as follows:

> 1953–1978
>
> The pleasure of your company is requested at
>
> The Silver Wedding Jubilee
>
> of
>
> Robert and Patricia Kring
>
> Saturday, the nineteenth of December
>
> at two o'clock
>
> 308 Carr Street
>
> Jackson, Michigan

You can also include the hosting information such as "The children of . . . invite you" or "Ed and Peggy Smith invite you to share in their tenth anniversary celebration with Tin-Can Charm." Be sure to mention the occasion as part of the event name or as a short blurb following it. For example, "Ninth Anniversary Potluck" or "A Groovy Leather Love-In Celebrating Jamie and Bonnie's Third Anniversary."

There's no need to worry extensively or study a course in invitation etiquette when designing your anniversary party invitation. If you have special concerns, consult your stationer for expert advice. Otherwise, plan to send invitations four to six weeks in advance. Include the why (anniversary year and party title), who (guests of honor and host), when (day, date, and time), and where (party site address). Enclose response cards with preaddressed and prestamped envelopes with formal invitations. For more casual affairs, an R.S.V.P. ("Répondez s'il vous plaît" or "please reply") printed on the invitation will do. I also find that adding a date and telephone number helps such as "R.S.V.P. by April 1, 517-555-5555."

When asking guests to bring or wear something special, personalize the message by enclosing a separate note with the invitation. For instance, you might handwrite a message on personal stationery asking guests to bring a verse, or you might include a photocopied message instead. You could also type a message several times on paper and cut it into small slips.

I've often used the term *engraved invitations* loosely in reference to printed invitations. True engraving is costly, as each invitation is hand pressed with a special plate. Professionally printed invitations are probably the most common. Thermography, my favorite, is a resin-and-heat process that leaves a raised-ink look on the paper. With today's advanced technology and beautiful laser papers, the home computer has become a popular tool for printing invitations that are appropriate for most anniversary parties. However, I would suggest professionally printed invitations for more formal and gala anniversary affairs.

It's also customary to place a milestone wedding anniversary announcement in your local newspaper (especially for twenty-five years, forty years, fifty years, sixty years, and so on). These announcements used to serve as an invitation to a small community affair, but today's announcement is more of a congratulatory gesture. In some regions, the announcement may be a news piece published free of charge. There's usually a form to complete at least four weeks in advance. Some newspapers will print photos of fifty-years-or-more anniversary couples and will take the photos in their studios. If the couple is infirm, the newspaper may send someone to the couple's home. Other newspapers treat this announcement as a classified advertisement and charge accordingly.

Anniversary Customs

Customs for formal anniversary celebrations, such as the "silver anniversary jubilee" and the "golden wedding anniversary," are similar to traditional wedding receptions. Some couples choose to reaffirm their commitment with specially written vows. Playing the couple's original wedding song for a first dance introduction is a favorite elegant custom. Many anniversary couples choose to duplicate the original wedding cake, flowers, and decorations as closely as possible for a romantic, nostalgic touch. Some even wear their original wedding clothes or use part of the lace or fabric in a new anniversary outfit. Reproducing wedding bouquet and boutonniere designs and carrying an original wedding accent (such as a gold pocket watch or wedding hankie) are sentimental touches.

In most cases, a wedding ceremony procession, veil and veil lifting, garter throwing, and rice tossing are not necessary. Nevertheless, a couple may want to include these customs in their anniversary celebration. Repeat wedding traditions tastefully. Consider giving the wedding tradition a contemporary "anniversary" twist. Display original wedding clothes at the anniversary party or have younger family members exhibit them in a fashion show. Some wedding customs have already evolved into modern party customs. For example, showering the wedding couple with rice as a symbol of fertility or an abundant life has evolved into the custom of showering any guest of honor with confetti. Look through the twenty-fifth and fiftieth wedding celebration chapters for more ideas on how celebration customs can be incorporated in your anniversary planning.

Many other popular wedding traditions are appropriate, sentimental reminders for a wedding anniversary. These include photos of the wedding party, anniversary programs, and a special prayer or blessing. Reception lines are very common, with the anniversary couple standing near the entrance, followed by their oldest to youngest children. It's also appropriate for any host to stand with the couple. Guests will feel welcomed when greeted as soon as they arrive. For elderly couples who might tire easily or are unable to stand, provide chairs or have other family members greet guests near the entrance. Also, formal reception lines are not necessary for smaller house parties. But it is always nice to have someone open the door for guests and to have the anniversary couple nearby to greet them.

For large formal receptions, the anniversary couple may be seated at a head table. Typically, they are seated either with original wedding party members or family members. Some couples would rather be seated with their guests. An ideal seating arrangement involves banquet tables placed in a horseshoe or open square pattern with guests seated on the outside rim. This allows the guests a view of the couple while giving the couple the feeling of sitting with all the guests. Work with your site manager to see what seating arrangement works best.

Another creative idea is to design a royal haven—a beautiful, intimate head table area exclusively for the husband and wife. Veil the anniversary couple in romantic privacy with a gazebo-like structure. Erect and decorate a lightweight, wrought iron or lattice-wood frame over a table set for two. Extend guest tables out from each end of this structure. Decorate the haven with royal splendor, adorning the chairs as thrones for the "king" and "queen." Continue the royal treatment by serving the anniversary couple with a private waiter, whose white-gloved service is only a footstep away.

Dancing is a very common anniversary festivity, although it doesn't always have to be included. Anniversary cake and a champagne (or sparkling cider) toast crown most anniversary celebrations. It's also common for guests to share individual toasts or anecdotes about the bride and groom at this time. Finally, capture anniversary memories with professional or amateur photography or videotaping.

Planning Basics

First, let me share the best event-planning advice I ever received: "Plan and coordinate every detail thoroughly and precisely but expect that some things will not unfold as planned—and accept this." Over the years, I've added my own planning motto: "Follow up, and follow up again!" I repeat these lines every time I plan a personal or professional event.

Planning and follow-up will reduce mistakes and mishaps. Make sure you have written agreements with all your product and service vendors. A written reference is a useful tool in helping clarify instructions and agreements. Call or meet with vendors to check on progress and clarify instructions before the event. ("Follow up, and follow up again!") If you are planning more than a month or two before the event, you may want to follow up between your initial meeting and the final follow-up. Always arrange for deliveries as soon as possible and check them thoroughly on the spot to allow time for correcting any shortages or mistakes.

No matter how hard we plan, the unexpected will most likely happen. Some undesirable situations (like the baker using lemon cream filling instead of raspberry, or Dad picking up pink instead of coral-colored napkins) are so minor guests won't notice. Don't say anything. But if something major happens, such as the beef roast burnt to a crisp or the tiered cake accidentally pushed over, don't panic. It's too late to start over or fix the situation, so just make the best of it. Order pizza and recruit an impromptu cleanup committee. Eating pizza and covering your guests with frosting weren't your original plans, but you'll enjoy laughing and talking about it until the next anniversary—and probably longer!

Anniversary Gifts

Guests have traditionally given gifts associated with the anniversary year. The couple may also choose to give each other gifts or buy themselves a special present. See Appendix A for the complete traditional and modern anniversary gift list. Contemporary theme-related suggestions are also included in each chapter. As a general rule, gifts should not be requested (the exception being an organized effort by family members and close friends). A family member may choose to coordinate the purchase of one large gift or shower the couple with items they like or need. Asking guests to bring a nominal gift (such as an inexpensive item to complete a set) or to bring an item that doesn't cost anything (like a composed verse) is not considered in bad taste, assuming it is done within a group of family and intimate friends.

Many people want or feel obligated to relay a "no gifts, please" message. I'm not fond of this custom. First, the message assumes guests intend to bring a gift. Second, the message creates a potentially awkward and confusing situation for guests, since some will bring gifts anyway. Let your guests decide whether to bring a gift. Gift giving pleases most people, and the anniversary couple should always accept gifts graciously. Requesting nominal or non-retail-value gifts can be a fun alternative to the "no gifts" request.

When possible, arrange for the anniversary couple to open any gifts in front of their guests. Accepting a gift is a compliment to the giver's generosity. He or she has made an effort to select and wrap just the right gift, and most givers will want to see the couple's response to their present. For frail or easily tired elderly couples, have younger family members open the gifts and present them to the couple. Gifts can also be opened and displayed on a table where the couple can enjoy looking at them.

Finally, older etiquette books often stated that giving money was not in good taste. Many objected to the suggested lack of thoughtfulness. However, some authors conceded, "If money must be given, display it in a creative and attractive manner." Today, monetary gifts are considered entirely appropriate—and are greatly appreciated. Guests can show added thoughtfulness by presenting the money in a creative manner such as displaying brand new bills in a gold card or folding them in a photo frame. Guests could also wrap the bills around the dangling hammer of a dinner bell or fold them to resemble leaves that are then attached to a branch or special tree decoration (the "money tree").

Planning and organizing party details are only the first steps in creating a successful and memorable wedding anniversary. Whether you're the host, the guest of honor, or both, the next step is to sit back and enjoy the moment. Don't let it pass you by. A wedding anniversary is a time of celebration—a happy and exciting time to share with your family and friends.

The First Anniversary
—Paper—

*Toast: Like indelible marks of ink on paper,
may your marriage record lifelong poetic fantasy!*

The first wedding anniversary commemorates the opening lines of a lifelong poetic union. The first year of marriage is delicate, like fine quality paper. Over the years, expressions of love will be indelibly written on the pages of married life.

The couple's first anniversary is particularly special. You'll want to celebrate the occasion with simple and delicate expression. Paper decorations are ideal for this situation and make party preparations very easy. They can be bought off the shelf and offer an endless array of paper anniversary themes. Each party can either be a romantic celebration for two or an intimate gathering of family and close friends from the wedding party.

Paper Picnic Poetics

Celebrate the paper anniversary with poetic splendor and inspiration: Create a romantic paper picnic.

Invitation Ideas

Send a poem inviting guests to help the couple celebrate their first year of married life:

> *An intimate paper picnic*
> *Of poetic splendor and cheer*
> *With a couple who's been married*
> *For one very happy year.*

Write the poem by hand on the outside of one of the following:

- White or brown paper lunch sack
- Hand-cut string of paper dolls or a commercial paper doll
- Small piece of clothing-pattern paper
- "Personals" section of a newspaper (List a telephone number for guests to call. Record a message with party details at this number. For security purposes, do not use actual addresses, which you should mail or phone to the guests.)
- Lovely piece of personal stationery
- Romantic paperback novel
- Paper airplane
- Handmade note card (Cut out dainty roses or other flowers from gift-wrap paper and glue to the outside of folded cardstock.)
- Victorian scrap (These are crafts from the Victorian era. Ladies tore pretty pictures from books or magazines and pasted them into scrapbooks. They also hung these cutouts on Christmas trees.)
- Small card attached to a tissue honeycomb bell
- Origami figure
- Boatlike paper hat, folded from newspaper

Special Instructions for Guests

Invite guests to bring a composed verse or copy of a favorite poem for the anniversary couple. Or, ask guests to bring books they've read or would like to read and include inscriptions telling why the couple would enjoy the books.

Decorating Touches

Set the picnic up under a shady tree in the park or in your backyard. Hang various-sized honeycomb bells from tree branches to catch the breeze. A romantic indoor setting can also be created in front of a warm fire or under soft candlelight. Next, set out your paper picnic area using the wedding colors. (Note: When celebrating outdoors, secure decorations with small rocks. Also, lay a blanket or plastic sheeting under the tablecloth to protect it from dampness.)

- Lay out a paper wedding-design tablecloth on the ground or floor.
- Add a picnic basket filled with paper plates, paper cups, and plastic silverware.
- Decorate the paper plates by gluing paper doilies and decorative accents to their centers. Use an anniversary card front or cut out a flower, heart, or romantic saying from wrapping paper.
- Place a paper centerpiece in the middle of the tablecloth using one of the following:
  —Decorative paper cups filled with fresh or tissue paper flowers
  —Wicker basket arranged with handmade paper flowers or wrapping-paper flower cutouts attached to pipe-cleaner stems
  —Papier-mâché statues or art pieces
  —Wedding-theme honeycomb centerpiece decorations
  —Stacks of love letters tied with a ribbon
- Decorate with a special newspaper theme display. Lay out newspapers for the tablecloth and add black and white paperware accents. Protect guests from the ink by covering the newspaper with a clear plastic tablecloth or thin plastic sheeting.

Theme-Inspired Activities and Entertainment

Reminisce with each other about the wedding's special moments and create new memories.

- Look through wedding photos, scrapbooks, and cards.
- Play any videotaped memories.
- Take turns reading aloud romantic verses from a book of poems.

- Share some poetic fantasy by reciting the poems brought by guests for the anniversary couple.
- Compose a poem together, each person adding a line of poetry. Consider having the anniversary couple start by completing the first few lines from Elizabeth Barrett Browning's classic love poem "How Do I Love Thee? Let Me Count the Ways."
- Conduct an old-fashioned box (or paper bag) lunch auction in which each guest bids on the box lunch of his or her choice. Supply decorated boxes or ask each guest to bring one to the auction beforehand. It's also fun to decorate the boxes or paper bags on site. Donate the auction proceeds to the couple for a dinner for two at their favorite restaurant.
- Play soft recordings of the wedding ceremony and reception music. Include paper-themed songs in the repertoire such as the Beatles's "Paperback Writer."
- Shower the couple with paper wishes. Ask friends and family to send greeting cards to the anniversary couple.
- Ask each guest to bring a wrapped paperback book or book of poetry to trade. The books can be traded in a musical-chairs-like gift pass or a fun lottery. Pass out a number printed on a small piece of paper to each guest. The person with number one starts by choosing any wrapped book. The person with number two follows, choosing either an unopened book or the book just opened by number one. This procedure repeats until the last gift is retrieved. To even out the chances, establish a rule that a book may be traded only three times.
- For romantic twosome-only picnics, hire a violin soloist to serenade the anniversary couple.
- Ceremoniously share the top layer of the wedding cake saved from the wedding.

Menu Ideas

Pack a picnic basket of toteable picnic fare:
- Crusty French bread served with Brie, pâté, and fruit preserves
- Crispy fried chicken drumsticks
- Asparagus in a raspberry vinaigrette
- Summer pasta or rice salad

- Top layer of wedding cake (saved from the wedding reception) or a special "Happy First Anniversary" cake
- Chilled bottle(s) of champagne for a celebratory toast

Party Favors with Flair

Include a touch of paper picnic poetics in each box lunch or distribute one from the picnic basket to each guest. Print one of the following inspirational words on elegant white card stock tied with a pretty satin ribbon or cord: patience, courage, promise, sharing, love, and so on. Or, attach a romantic poem to one of the following paper mementos:

- Scented personal stationery or note card, tied with a pretty ribbon
- A bouquet of tissue paper roses or a single paper flower
- Romantic paperback novel
- Origami figure
- Victorian scrap memento
- Papier-mâché figure
- Paper knife (the Victorian phrase for letter opener)
- Decorative paper weight

It's a Wonderful Life
Paper Romance

Decorate with *It's a Wonderful Life* honeymoon romance. Remember in the movie when Mary transformed the old, run-down Grandville house into a romantic resort for her honeymoon? After the run on the bank, George and Mary gave up their honeymoon trip around the world. So Mary invited George to come home to 320 Sycamore—"The Waldorf Hotel." She creatively decorated around cobwebs and roof leaks to bring home the wish George had made years before: to "see the world—Italy, Greece, the Parthenon, the Coliseum."

Like Mary, you can transform an everyday house into a romantic resort by hanging travel posters of Florida, the South Pacific, Hawaii, or the couple's particular dream destination. Decorate the table with a paper tablecloth and tropical honeycomb decorations. Add romantic candlelight, the top layer of wedding cake (saved from the wedding reception) with its original cake topper, and a silver bucket of chilled champagne. Hang tropical paper decorations from the ceiling and on the walls. If you like, add cobwebs and drip-catching pails around the room. You might also create a vignette (or crude drawing) of the gramophone-and-pulley setup Mary used to roast two chickens in the fireplace.

Invite guests by sending details attached to a travel brochure or by a phone call. Greet guests with a handwritten "Honeymoon Suite" sign hung on the outside of the door. Then have an Ernie-the-cab-driver character greet guests by tipping his top hat and saying, "Entrez, Monsieur (or Madam)." Inside play mood-inspiring Hawaiian music. Then have the Ernie-the-cab-driver and Burt-the-cop characters serenade the anniversary couple with the ballad "I Love You Truly," just like in the movie. End this romantic adventure by viewing a taped version of the classic movie.

It's Only a Paper Moon!

Hang a paper moon and celebrate under its romantic glow. Chinese cultures celebrate the Moon Festival with moonlit picnics, eating moon cakes (round cakes filled with red bean paste, lotus seed paste, or coconut) and telling fables about the lady who lives in the moon. What a wonderful way to spend a first anniversary!

In addition, make each guest a sky-gazing device. Take a paper cup and draw a constellation configuration, such as the Big Dipper or Cassiopeia, on the outside bottom of the cup. Then poke a hole, using a straight pin or thumbtack, in the center of each star. Shine a flashlight through the cup to project the image onto a wall or ceiling of a darkened room.

Next, sing moon-inspired songs such as "Moon River," "Shine on Harvest Moon," "Moonlight and Roses," "There's a New Moon Over My Shoulder," and, of course, "It's Only a Paper Moon." Cap off the night under the paper moon by wishing on floating candles. Make floating candles by melting candle wax into empty walnut shell halves. Stick a birthday candle upright in the middle of the wax, letting it cool and set. Then burn the birthday candles while floating the walnuts in a large bowl of water. Have each guest make a paper moon anniversary wish and blow out one of the candles.

Take a Paper Holiday

Take guests on a paper holiday with a trip around the world. Use paper decorations to set up buffet tables as different international or period sites. Decorate one table with Mexican flair using paper piñatas, cactus cutouts, and brightly colored tableware. Serve colored tortilla chips with spicy guacamole and salsa dips, miniburritos, a make-your-own taco bar, and frozen margaritas. Hang one of the piñatas and blindfold players, one at a time, for some piñata-breaking fun. Decorate another buffet table with an Italian theme, using Italian flags, a red-and-white-checked paper tablecloth, and paper cut-out decorations picturing gondoliers or the Leaning Tower of Pisa. Use Italian wine bottles with basket-weave bases as the centerpiece. Drip colorful wax over a taper candle placed in the bottlenecks. Play beautiful opera music and serve a variety of pasta salads, a mixed green salad with Italian dressing, and Italian ices, cappuccinos, and espressos.

Expand your travel itinerary with adventurous time travel. Accelerate beyond the current time barrier by sending guests into the future with a sci-fi table covered in shiny metallic paper. Place life-sized cardboard figures of well-known galaxy characters, such as Darth Vader or Captain Kirk, next to the table. Take instant photos of guests standing next to these figures and give guests Milky Way and Mars candy bar favors. Travel back in time with a fifties rock-and-roll station decorated with paper records hanging over pink, black, and turquoise-colored paper tableware. Have a soda jerk or carhop character on roller skates serve hamburgers and French fries on paper plates. Also, add cherry cokes and chocolate malts to this nostalgic menu. Whatever destinations you end up choosing, guests are sure to experience a memorable paper holiday.

Anniversary Gift Suggestions

Choose one of these very special paper anniversary gifts:

- Blank journal to record love thoughts, poems, and special memories
- Romantic book of poetry or other gift book
- Decorative box to keep love letters, cards, and notes
- Personally composed poem written on delicate stationery
- Paper coupons

- Paper Christmas ornament (Consider giving the couple a new ornament to add to their collection each anniversary year.)
- Watercolor print
- Paperhanger and gift certificate for wallpapering a room in the couple's house
- Paper money folded and placed in a decorative photo frame
- Stock certificate that represents a share or shares of a company stock purchased for the couple
- Magazine subscription
- Clock or the movie *Somewhere in Time* with Christopher Reeve (The anniversary gift charts often list clocks as the modern first anniversary gift designation. The clock signifies a time to love, time spent with each other, and a timeless treasure.)

A Special Moment for the Anniversary Couple

A Romantic Paper Trail

Leave a romantic paper trail for your spouse. Write enticing messages on single pieces of scented stationery, leading your spouse on a path of alluring adventure. Leave each note in a strategic location, lighted by a single candle and decorated with scattered rose petals. The first note guides your spouse to the stereo that is ready to play mood-inspiring music. The next note leads to two toasting glasses and a bottle of champagne. The next note leads to a softly lit candlelight dinner for two. After dinner, a note directs the reader to thick plush towels laid out before a rose-scented bath. Finally, the last note leads to a single rose and a book of romantic poetry laid upon your spouse's pillow.

The Second Anniversary
—Cotton—

Toast: Here's to wrapping yourselves in cottony-soft love!

After two years of marriage, the couple's lives are becoming comfortably interwoven. It seems appropriate, then, to celebrate with pure, natural cotton, the traditional second anniversary gift. Cotton brings to mind soft cloth, pillowy blooms, and weaving looms. Cotton also reminds us of the Southern charm of cotton plantations and cotton gins. With a little imagination, simple items such as a cotton kitchen apron can inspire great anniversary themes. Events like the Cotton Bowl or movies like *The Cotton Club* can be developed into wonderful cotton anniversary ideas.

The "Cotton Club" Anniversary Show

Recreate the thrill of the original posh Cotton Club with an intimate nightclub atmosphere, featuring the unrivaled excitement of jazz rhythms. Rub shoulders with the romantic memory of the original Harlem Cotton Club. During the roaring twenties and early thirties, the club's owner, "Owney" Madden (rumored leader of the notorious Gopher Gang), showcased legendary stars such as Duke Ellington, Cab Calloway, and Lena Horne. It was the hottest spot in town for both rich and poor, celebrities and gangsters. Borrow a bit of this excitement to create your Cotton Club anniversary fun.

Invitation Ideas

Invite guests to The "Cotton Club" Anniversary Show with an engraved invitation along with one of following jazz items or designs:

- Fluffy cotton balls placed inside a cellophane bag, tied with a decorative ribbon
- Small vintage evening bag
- Monogrammed terry cloth hand towel
- Piece of decorative cotton cloth
- Black top hat (paper or cloth)
- Cotton Club program reproduction
- Jazz era sheet music cover
- Early jazz period album cover
- Jazz cassette tape or CD
- Post card or photo of a Cotton Club star such as Cab Calloway

Special Instructions for Guests

Invite guests to dress in elegant nightclub wear or vintage jazz-age costumes. If you're feeling rebellious and sassy, ask guests to come dressed in cotton pajamas.

Decorating Touches

Capture the legendary mystique of the Cotton Club by creating a jazz club atmosphere in your living room, an event room, or a room at a restaurant or nightclub. Design it with an underlying tone of gangster era swank:

- Hang a Cotton Club tent awning or sign at the party entrance.
- Roll out a long, narrow red carpet.
- Have a costumed doorman greet guests at the club entrance.
- Cover tables with crisp white cotton tablecloths.

- Float a beautiful damask rose in a large brandy snifter as a fragrant centerpiece.

- Make a soft centerpiece sculpture using men's white cotton dress gloves. Arrange a pair of outstretched "hands" (gloves stuffed with cotton batting) inside a formal black top hat (cloth or paper). If you like, add glittering silver-colored cut-out shapes to the gloves, placing the decoration inside the palms or between the forefinger and thumb. The "hands" will look as if they are holding a musical note, musical instrument, or "CC" shape (for Cotton Club). To support the "hands," place a stiff pipe cleaner inside the glove and through the batting. Then poke the bottom end of the pipe cleaner into a floral block. Conceal the top of the block and base of the gloves with decorative Mylar grass.

- A similar but easier arrangement can be made by laying a pair of men's white cotton gloves over the rim of a top hat. Drape a red tuxedo scarf around the base of the top hat and add a black-cane accent. Finally, lay a single red rose at each place setting as an elegant statement. Alternate this arrangement with another high fashion expression. Set a lady's high-heeled shoe on a circular mirror with a soft glowing votive candle. Drape a string of faux pearls over the edge of the shoe. Then, as an optional decoration, add a fluffy white feather boa.

- Create a soft, glowing ambiance with small candles or small vintage table lamps.

- Fit black cotton T-shirts over chair backs. Imprint each shirt with silver lettering reading, "Joe and Julie's Cotton Club Second Anniversary Show."

- Serve bottles of champagne from elaborate silver champagne coolers placed on floor stands.

- Rope off the dance floor to create an entertainment stage. Cover the dance floor with metallic silver, black, and white balloons.

- Set up chairs and music stands at the end of the dance floor or stage to create an area for the band.

Theme-Inspired Activities and Entertainment

Saturate the evening with exciting jazz music and one or two Cotton-Club-inspired ideas. Or, go all out and stage a dinner-dance show with Cotton-Club-like revues bursting with riveting entertainment: jazz singers, tap dancers, glamorous dancing girls, vaudeville performers, and comics.

- Hire gangster-costumed characters to provide walk-around greeting entertainment.
- Have a cigarette girl, dressed in early thirties fashion, walk around and pass out candy cigarettes and cigars. Place the favors in a vintage-looking box tray that hangs from a strap wrapped around the back of her neck.
- Invite guests to lip-synch jazz era songs.
- Give a megaphone to the master of ceremonies to make nostalgic comments, introductions, and announcements.
- Offer karaoke entertainment and videotape the performances.
- Recruit friends and family to stage a talent show with song and dance routines and comedy acts.
- Hire a professional to give the crowd tap-dancing lessons.
- Show the movie *Cotton Club,* starring Richard Gere.
- Play blues and jazz recordings of artists from the Cotton Club era.
- To add an informal, novel touch, conduct a high-heeled shoe and tie check at the door. Store the items in a coat-check room and pass out cotton slippers for the ladies' comfort.
- Have a period-costumed roving photographer take instant photos of guests while they're seated at their tables. Also, if possible, give the photographer a vintage flash bulb camera prop.
- Set up an area to look like an old-fashioned remote radio broadcast. Place a vintage microphone prop with an "NBC" logo on one of the guest tables. Then have a DJ "radio broadcaster" (dressed in a late twenties or early thirties suit and hat) play jazz tunes from a small sound system on the table.
- Have tuxedo-clad waiters deliver martinis to guests at their tables. Martinis mark the time when gin's shady "bathtub" past had a sexy

quality, and society types were rubbing shoulders with known gangsters while listening to the dangerous rhythms of jazz.

- Coordinate an old-fashioned cakewalk. Have contestants compete in "Take the cake!" dancing, showing their most imaginative struts. Many of the zany moves in original cakewalks included fancy steps that are now standard in tap-dancing repertoires.

Menu Ideas

Indulge guests with a bountiful soul food buffet:

- Showcase a wide selection of main dishes including crispy fried chicken, smoked pork sausage, barbecued riblets, baked pecan chicken breasts with creole mustard, ham hocks smothered in red-eyed gravy, and braised turkey wings.
- Add a variety of tantalizing side dishes including fresh string beans, sautéed chicken livers, chitterlings, collard greens, black-eyed peas, extra cheesy baked macaroni and cheese, red beans and rice, and barbecued black beans.
- Lay out plenty of salad, soup, and bread choices including southern beet salad, tossed green salad, potato salad, creole chicken gumbo, homemade corn bread, buttermilk biscuits, steaming hot dinner rolls, and hush puppies.
- Top off the buffet with mouth-watering desserts including spoon bread, sweet potato pie, real southern banana pudding, blueberry cobbler, and a decadent sour cream chocolate anniversary cake.

Party Favors with Flair

Select a party favor with Cotton Club mystique such as the cotton T-shirts used as chair covers (see *Decorating Touches*) or jazz tapes or CDs. These cotton-inspired gifts also make lovely mementos:

- Monogrammed cotton hankies (Use the "CC" for Cotton Club or personalize the monogram for each guest.)
- A cotton-scarf-wrapped flowerpot gathered with a pretty ribbon and filled with a cotton-ball plant or other plant
- A dainty cotton hankie filled with bath scents, gathered and tied with a pretty ribbon (You might add the note "A comfort to your tired dancing feet.")

- A delicate, white cotton pillow filled with lavender, cinnamon, and chamomile (You might attach lines from Percy Shelley's poem "The Cloud" such as "And all the night 'tis my pillow white, / While I sleep . . . Sublime on the towers of my skiey bowers."
- Soft cotton socks
- Cotton candy
- Plush cottontail bunny toy

Apron Cookin' Fun

One can further spin the cotton theme by sending each guest a cotton apron or chef's hat silk-screened with party invitation details. Vintage kitchen aprons (pockets filled with invitations) make an especially clever statement. Hold this fun, informal second anniversary celebration right in your kitchen! Set the mood by complementing the menu with appropriate music. For instance, serve guests a glass of full-bodied wine while playing dramatic Italian operas and cooking up an amoré-inspiring spaghetti meal. Or, put on some snappy martini lounge music and serve classic cocktails while preparing a chic gourmet meal. Work together by assigning each guest a specific cooking task—the perfect recipe for kitchen cooking fun.

A Cotton Bowl Anniversary Party

Gather a team of friends and family together to kick off the couple's second anniversary with a sporty Cotton Bowl party. Decorate the area in wedding team colors and distribute cotton T-shirt uniforms imprinted with the team's name (Cotton Bowl Lovers) and player number (2). The game plan for this party includes touch football and a tailgate picnic served from car trunks. You might stage some entertaining half-time festivities such as conducting a Cotton Bowl Parade of anniversary gifts or showing a recording of last year's Cotton Bowl game. It'll be a real "Touchdown!" anniversary celebration!

Anniversary Gift Suggestions

The traditional gift of cotton lends itself to many comfy second anniversary gifts:

- Matching terry cotton robes
- Monogrammed terry bath towels
- Cotton pillow autographed by party guests
- His-and-her cotton sweaters or crisp cotton shirts
- Set of cotton sheets
- Cotton throw (a knitted or crocheted afghan) personalized with the couple's names and anniversary date
- Patchwork quilt or wall hanging made from cotton fabric pieces
- Pillow made with fluffy, tufted vintage chenille fabric
- Book on the Cotton Club, cotton plantations, cotton gins, or cotton weaving
- China teapot or a new or replacement piece of china for the couple's china pattern (China is the modern gift designation listed on most anniversary gift charts.)

A Special Moment for the Anniversary Couple

A Cottony-Soft Pampering Spa

Wrap your spouse in anniversary pampering. Hide away at a luxury hotel, transforming your private suite into a special cottony-soft pampering spa just for the two of you. Draw a hot bath and season it with the relaxing comfort of sea salts. Then dry off in large, thick terry cotton towels. Play your favorite music and light aromatherapy candles to fill the room with comforting calm. Wrap up in cozy cotton robes and treat each other to a manicure. Then, using a natural bristle brush, take turns gently brushing each other's hair. Continue the pampering spa treatment with tender and therapeutic massages. Order room service for martinis or cappuccinos—or even milk and cookies. Then cuddle up in a cotton blanket with your loved one and the daily paper, a novel, or a favorite movie for an evening of total comfort.

The Third Anniversary
—Leather—

*Toast: May your marriage be a leather-strong
protective covering for your love!*

L eather, the traditional third anniversary gift, is often used for protection against the elements. Marriage offers similar protection
for new and growing relationships. The third-anniversary couple,
increasingly secure in their strengthening alliance, is ready to have a
little leather fun.

A Ride on the Wild Side

The motorcycle was born to defy convention. Take a ride on the wild
side with this leather-clad anniversary celebration. Drop out of the
conventional Establishment, just for a night, and take an easy ride into
this unique biker anniversary celebration.

Invitation Ideas

Invite guests with "motorcycle-mama" daring:

- Print invitation ideas on officially licensed Harley Davidson invitations or post cards.

- Choose a greeting card or post card with leather-clad bikers or
  motorcycle photos.

- Paste invitation details onto a folded road map, tying each with a narrow strip of leather.
- Send leather motorcycle hats with the invitations.
- Send a bandanna and the lyrics to "Born to Be Wild." (See the *Theme-Inspired Activities and Entertainment* section for information on how to use this prop.)

Special Instructions for Guests

Dress on the wild side and wear your "leathers" including leather jackets, pants, skirts, biker hats, motorcycle boots, and any other piece of leather clothing desired.

Decorating Touches

Decorate the area in truck-stop or biker-bar style or hold the party in a bar or at a truck stop restaurant. (Hint: Unless you're a bona fide biker, stay away from real biker bars, which can be rough. Create your biker bar atmosphere in a more sedate bar or party room.)

- Have bouncers, one dressed as a burly doorman and one as a motorcycle mama, greet guests at the entrance.
- Set up a Harley Hog (motorcycle) by the jukebox and ham it up for instant-photo favor opportunities.
- Line the walls with temporary shelves that hold rows and rows of Budweiser beer bottles.
- Hang Harley Davidson leather jackets, advertising signs, T-shirts, and other memorabilia on the walls.
- Add neon beer advertisements to the wall décor.
- For some wild prankster fun, reverse restroom signs. Hang a "Motorcycle Mamas" sign outside the men's room and a "Big Burly Biker" sign outside the women's room.
- Park hogs on tabletops (the fat, pink kind this time). Start by covering tabletops with flat, unfolded road maps. Then place a leather square over the center of the map. Finally, place toy hogs (pigs) on top of the leather square. Dress the hogs with biker accents such as leather jackets and bandannas around their foreheads.
- Decorate with Harley Davidson licensed paperware and balloons, now available from local party suppliers.

Theme-Inspired Activities and Entertainment

As "leader of the pack," take guests on a joy ride they won't forget.

- Play the movie *Easy Rider* on a large screen over the dance floor.
- Hire a live rock-and-roll dance band.
- Provide "king of the road" interactive entertainment such as motorcycle video games or virtual computer games.
- Hold a karaoke contest in which guests dress up as tough, leather-clad bikers and sing silly children's songs or country music ballads. The contrast between persona and music will be hilarious.
- Organize a "hog toss." Set up targets, such as hanging rubber tires, empty beer cans, and score-marked empty beer cartons, at one end of the bar. Then have bikers toss their "hogs" (plush pig toys, pig beanbags, or rubber pigs) at the targets.
- Hold a "sexiest biker legs" contest with guys only as contestants.
- Place a huge jar of motorcycle parts on the end of the bar. Encourage biker guests to guess the number of parts in the jar and award a prize to the winner.
- Place various motorcycle parts and auto tools on the tabletops. Hold up the parts and tools one by one and award points or prizes to the guests who correctly identify the items.
- Toast the anniversary couple with bottled beer.
- Pass out bandanna headbands and the lyrics to "Born to Be Wild" to each guest. On cue, have the guests put on the headbands and sing to the anniversary couple.
- Stage a motorcycle parade and give guests motorcycle rides.
- Conduct a "tough and burly" tricycle race.

Menu Ideas

Guests will be in hog heaven with these mouth-watering roadside recipes. Try any of the following truck stop favorites:

- "Hot as Hell" chicken wings
- Biker-sized portions of barbecued pork ribs, fried chicken, meat loaf, smoked link sausages, and chicken-fried steak

- "Hogtail" curly French fries and unlimited mashed potatoes—both smothered in gravy
- Steaming hot corn on the cob and black-eyed peas with ham hocks
- Freshly baked sweet cornbread with honey butter
- Heaping portions of chocolate anniversary cake and homemade pies
- Lots of strong black coffee

Party Favors with Flair

No bike trip is complete without collecting a Harley Davidson T-shirt imprinted with the city's name. So for this special occasion, provide a Harley Davidson T-shirt imprinted with "Ron and Karen's Third Anniversary—Denver, Colorado." Other wild party favor ideas include the following:

- Harley Davidson key chains or other licensed memorabilia
- Hogs (toy pigs)
- Bandannas from the singing skit described in the *Entertainment* section
- CDs or cassette tapes of "Born to Be Wild"
- Temporary tattoos (You might provide a shot of tequila for each customer before beginning the tattooing process.)

Boot-Kickin' Anniversary Fun

Saddle up for some boot-kickin' anniversary fun. It's time for dressing in leather cowboy hats, leather boots and chaps, and overall western garb. Bring in some bales of hay and hang a leather saddle, a horse bridle, and other western tack over a split rail fence. Then get in the "moo-d" by covering tables with cowhide print cloths. Alternate table centerpieces made with a single leather boot or leather cowboy hat filled with yellow daisies, bright sunflowers, or multicolored wildflowers. For table favors, cover baby-food jars with bandannas and fill with fresh gypsophila. Tie leather laces around their rims and around red bandanna napkins.

Then cook up a chuck wagon supper with open-fire-cooked steaks, barbecued chicken, steak fries, corn on the cob, and baked beans. For dessert, bake a cake with old west flavor—a cowboy anniversary coffee cake branded with the couple's initials. Serve it with tin or enamel-ware mugs of strong black coffee. Entertain guests with the harmony and yodeling of cowboy campfire music. Then it's time to kick up your heels with the laughter of cowboy poet humor. Later in the evening, haul out long-neck beer bottles from ice tubs placed in a ribbon-trimmed old-fashioned country wagon. Add a covered wagon awning if you like. It's time for some two-stepping fun. Tear up the dance floor with those leather boots. Hold an old-fashioned square dance or hire a DJ to teach the Texas two-step and other popular line dances.

A Leather-Bound Classic Tale

This is a classic tale of storybook romance. Think of the smell of leather-bound books and the quiet ambiance of library romance. This party will tell the story of two people deeply in love and their passion for classic literature. About six to eight weeks before the anniversary date, send close friends and relatives an invitation to meet and discuss a classic tale. For this novel anniversary celebration, send leather-bound copies of a chosen work such as Jane Austen's *Pride and Prejudice* or Shakespeare's *Romeo and Juliet.* As an economical alternative, cover an inexpensive hardback version of the book with folded book jackets cut from a single piece of leather cloth. Ask guests to read the story in advance of the book-discussion dinner.

Meet in the private room of a stylish restaurant to discuss the book in detail. Serve vintage wine and seat guests in comfortable high-back chairs around an elegantly set table for an evening of prose and conversation. Start by reciting the following literary toast: "To the Homely Three—A good book, a bright light, and an easy chair."

A Groovy Leather Love-In

In the late fifties, leather symbolized the teenage rebellion that contrasted dramatically with the innocent early fifties. Leather jackets were made popular by famous screen idols such as James Dean and Marlon Brando. The sixties brought us Mod fashions, but a defiant rival movement, known in England as The Rockers, protested the Mods by wearing trademark leather jackets, leather motorcycle boots, and crash helmets. And the rock-and-roll era began with a bad-boy, leather-jacket image made popular by Elvis Presley. In the late sixties, leather took on a seductive Barbarella look in movie costumes. Soon after, groovy leather jumpers, leather miniskirts, and patent leather go-go boots hit the discotheques.

Hold a groovy leather love-in reflecting the fashions of this period. Invite guests to wear leather fashion statements from the fifties and sixties. Get out the leather-look beanbag chairs and plug in the psychedelic lights and lava lamps. Dance to music that reflects the rebellious mood of the times. Hold a contest for the hippest, grooviest, and most far-out costume. Don't forget to photograph this anniversary love-in to preserve some really cool memories.

Anniversary Gift Suggestions

Consider his-and-her Harley Davidson jackets as a biker-themed gift or one of these leather gift statements:

- Leather gloves or boots
- Leather-bound classic book
- Matching leather Daytimers
- Leather luggage
- Leather photo album
- Leather belt, handbag, or moccasins
- Leather camera bag containing a camera to capture anniversary memories
- Crystal figurines, crystal wine goblets, or a crystal bowl (Crystal, the modern gift designation, perfectly reflects the crystal clear love the couple shares for each other.)

A Special Moment for the Anniversary Couple

"Me Tarzan, you Jane!"

Plan an evening on the wild side. Dress in animal leather skins (animal-print-patterned lingerie) and snuggle up to a Tarzan movie accompanied by your own monkeyshines.

The Fourth Anniversary
—Fruit and Flowers—

Toast: May your future be filled with wine and roses!

Traditionally, the fourth anniversary is immersed in the enchanting fragrance of flowers and the sweet taste of fruit. Flowers and fruit have a timeless quality and are universally welcomed gift-giving expressions. A flower blooms and fruit ripens like new and growing love. Thus, the fourth anniversary should be celebrated with the loving, heartfelt expression of fruit and flowers.

A Charming Fruit-and-Flowers Garden Party

Invite guests to come to a garden party immersed in fruit and flower charm. This delightful anniversary celebration is the perfect excuse for wearing fabulous hats and nostalgic gloves while keeping the genteel company of the opposite sex. The host receives garden guests on the lawn, in a flower garden, on a garden patio, or in a charming indoor garden setting.

Invitation Ideas

Here are some bloomin' ideas for creative fruit or floral invitations:

- Send guests a note attached to a pretty garden glove.
- Send invitation details along with a fresh piece of fruit or attach them to a plastic or silk replica. If you like, glue fruit-colored glass beads to plastic fruit pieces before sending.
- Deliver a single fresh flower, such as a white rose, or send a silk flower through the mail. Include a note explaining its symbolism. For example, a white rose signifies charm and innocence.
- Send a handwritten note on pressed-flower stationery or flower-design note cards.
- Roll the invitation into a tubular shape and slip it through an empty flower seed packet slit at both ends.

Special Instructions for Guests

Ask guests to bring a single silk flower for the anniversary couple. As guests arrive, collect the flowers into a pretty vase as a lasting memento for the anniversary couple.

Decorating Touches

Flowers and fruit will create a lovely ambiance for the party. This verse by Leigh Hunt expresses the mood well: "Colors are the smiles of nature . . . they are her laughs, as in flowers." Try one or more of these garden party decorations:

Fabulous Fruity and Floral Inspiration Centerpieces

- Make a flower cake centerpiece. Form a cake shape with mesh wire around a cake pan. Remove the pan and fill the wire form with flowers. Display your flowery creation on a china or glass cake stand.
- Make a sunny-looking fruity flower vase. Simply slice oranges, lemons, and limes in half and place them inside a glass container with the insides facing out. Then fill the container with water and place fresh-cut flowers in the center. A dry centerpiece can also be made by placing a small tubular vase inside a larger bowl-like vase.

Fill the inside vase with water and a floral bouquet while placing fruit between the inside and outside vase.

- Make an unusual antique floral statement, planting flowers in an old boot or in a flower "bed" (made by planting flowers inside a vintage doll bed).
- Cut a watermelon in half and hollow out its center. Then arrange flowers in this unique centerpiece vase.
- Pile oranges, tangerines, and kumquats into a crystal bowl. Then stick yellow roses and bay leaves between the fruit.
- Arrange flowerpots of geraniums or other annual flowers in the center of the table.
- Place tulips or daffodils in a watering can.
- Group antique teacups together, each planted with fresh grass and flowers, for a fetching centerpiece.
- Fill a gingham-covered fruit jar with fragrant lilacs. Tie the jar with a beautiful satin ribbon.

Fruit and Floral Table Accents

- Carve a small circular hole in the top of an orange or apple to hold a small votive candle.
- Make a pretty floral impression by pressing fresh flowers between two glass plates, blooms facing up.
- Slip napkins though flower seed packet napkin rings made by slitting both ends of an empty seed packet.
- Place silverware and napkins in novel flowerpot buffet holders.
- Provide warmed, rose-water-scented finger towels.
- Decorate place cards with small blooms.
- Make fruity place card holders using lemons or limes. Make a small slit on the top of the fruit and then slip the place card into this surprise holder.
- Lay a single fresh flower at each place setting. Tie each stem with a small card explaining the meaning of the flower. For instance,

> —Aster: Elegance
>
> —Carnation (red): Admiration
>
> —Carnation (white): Pure and ardent love
>
> —Chrysanthemum (white): Truth

—Daffodil: Regard

—Daisy: Innocence

—Pansy: Thoughtful recollection

—Forget-me-not: Friendship

—Geranium (red): Comfort

—Iris: Faith, wisdom, valor

—Lily of the Valley: Purity

—Rose (red): Love

—Rose (yellow): Jealousy

—Rose (white): Charm

—Sunflower: Devotion

- Make a centerpiece arrangement using both flowers and whole fruit.

Garden Party Area Accents

- Hang a pineapple, long a traditional symbol of hospitality, on the front door or gatepost.
- Set out arrangements of colorful birdhouses, birdbaths, and bird feeders around the garden to attract feathery creatures.
- Set out benches and hang a hammock in the shade for lazy garden reflections. Watch the clouds roll by or close your eyes and listen to the sounds of nature: birds chirping, bees buzzing, and the wind singing.
- Fill a redwood or metal child's wagon with clay pots of geraniums and other annuals.
- Hang a tree swing decorated with flower garlands.

Theme-Inspired Activities and Entertainment

These fruit and flower activities are easy to bring to fruition:

- As a fun table mixer, give one of the flowers listed in the *Decorating Touches* section to each guest as he or she arrives. Ask each guest to locate the flower's corresponding meaning printed on a small card placed at one of the place settings.

- Place a flower or fruit-design friendship card under each plate. Let guests know that the holder of the card containing a flower petal (one at each table) takes the centerpiece home.
- Seat the flower girl from the wedding in the guest of honor seat, introducing her to guests with a special toast.
- Hold an old-fashioned croquet or lawn bowling tournament with flower-garland-wrapped mallets, using oranges as balls.
- Throw horseshoes or lawn darts.
- Entertain guests with a harpist or string quartet.
- Recite verses from a book of flower poems.
- Make flower garland necklaces.

Menu Ideas

Create an unforgettable anniversary garden or luncheon fantasy, selecting your fruity and floral accents from this bouquet of menu ideas:

Fruity Delights
- Baked Brie with strawberry glaze served with crusty French bread and large ripe strawberries
- Pâté on green apple slices
- Mandarin orange and spinach salad
- Strawberry soup
- Ham and pineapple-salad finger sandwiches
- Orange-glazed, coconut-fried drumsticks
- Broiled chicken breasts with lime
- Fruit pizza
- Pineapple tree with fresh fruit kabobs served with a strawberry-honey dip
- Fruit salad
- Hollowed oranges filled with raspberry sherbet
- An assortment of fruit tarts and lemon crunch cookies
- Pitchers of homemade lemonade with rose-petal ice cubes
- Guava champagne punch with rose and fruit ice mold

Floral Fantasies

- Stuffed tulips (Remove the inside stem, then wash and air dry the inside of the tulips. Fill with egg salad and enjoy.)
- Fresh garden vegetables served with bleu cheese dip and garnished with edible flowers
- Open-faced rose- and violet-petal sandwiches made by pressing edible flowers into a cream cheese and rose water mixture
- Rosemary new potatoes
- Bread baked in flowerpots
- A rose-petal anniversary cake decorated with frosted fruit and flowers (Brush the outside of fruit, such as red grapes, with a tiny amount of lightly beaten egg white. Then sift a light dusting of sugar over the fruit and edible flowers.)
- Groom's cake, a traditional fruitcake placed in decorative take-home boxes (Remind guests that it is traditional to place the cake under their pillows to bring dreams of their loved ones.)
- Rose-petal tea

Party Favors with Flair

Send each guest home with a handmade garden gift blooming with sweet sentiment.

- Lacy hankie sachet filled with fragrant rosy red or lavender blue potpourri
- Garden tussie-mussie—a small bouquet of flowers decorated with ribbon and bits of lace or paper doilies (Like the Victorians, spell out a romantic message with your flower selections. For example, spell "love" with lavender, orchid, violets, and eucalyptus.)
- Box of homemade floral dusting powder made with four parts cornstarch and one part finely ground flowers
- Bottle of homemade lavender water or a bar of hand-milled rose-petal soap
- Decorative tin of homemade rose-and-oatmeal scrub
- Edible flower food such as a jar of rose-petal honey or violet jelly
- Flower-petal-trimmed photo frame

- Sugared marzipan fruit placed in a clear cellophane bag and tied with a pretty satin ribbon and a large delicate rose bloom
- Wire-flower-wrapped lipstick tube, package of chewing gum, or perfume bottle
- Fruit jar layered with lines of flower potpourri colors

Moonlight and Roses
Wine Tasting

Surrender to the spell of moonbeams and the permeating fragrance of the rose bloom. This luminous atmosphere presents an ideal setting for wine tasting and rose appreciation. Invite an intimate group of friends to celebrate the couple's fourth anniversary with charm and grandeur. If possible, hold the wine tasting outdoors under the moonlight. For cold or rainy weather, hold this enchanting gathering in a heated clear ceiling tent. Bring the outside in with leafy green potted trees encircled by tall, fragrant rose bushes. Add the romance of sheer white tulle fabric over twinkle lights, draping it from the ceiling center to the tent corners. Swirl strings of rose garlands over the tulle. Finally, wrap the tent columns with the same treatment of tulle twinkle lights and rose garlands.

For the table, this rose sentiment from Emma Goldman comes to mind: "I'd rather have roses on my table than diamonds on my neck." Start a masterpiece rose table treatment by covering a twelve- to eighteen-foot-long line of banquet tables with crisp white linens. Cover chairs with dramatic white chair covers and drape a thorn-free rose garland on each chair back. Form a line down the center of the table with tall silver candelabra stands holding dramatic white taper candles. Next, lay garlands of red roses down the table line, draping them up and over the bases of the candelabra stands. As a final touch, add bottles of the couple's private-label wine down this line to create a table of wine and roses. Private-label wine is available commercially (see the *Supplier Resource Directory*) or you can make your own by placing self-stick labels on the bottles. Add beautiful harp music to this perfect wine-tasting setting. Set up a telescope for moon- and stargazing. Then add dancing under the stars to the music of a string quartet to complete this rapturous moonlight and roses experience.

Flower Child Meadow Party

It's back to the flower child Twilight Zone of the sixties for a "make love not war" anniversary party. Ask guests to wear some flowers in their hair and don their psychedelic hippie duds. It's time to pull out those bell-bottom, hip-hugging blue jeans and macramé or leather-fringed vests. Don't forget the headbands, love beads, peace signs, and other far-out statements. Hold this nostalgic invocation of love, beauty, and peace in an idyllic meadow setting. Choose a grassy field or park in the great outdoors or create an indoor Woodstock ambiance.

Form a caravan to the party scene led by a psychedelic-painted Volkswagen Bus. The flower-and-peace-sign-painted bus can serve as the area centerpiece. Or, hang a sign decorated with a drawing of a psychedelic-painted bus to a lead car. Add tents, large peace-sign paintings, and antiwar banners to decorate the area. Cover tables with bright tie-dyed tablecloths. Add napkins in bright psychedelic colors such as chartreuse, lemon yellow, neon orange, lime green, and grape. Wrap the napkins with love beads and a pair of granny glasses. Place daisies in empty wine bottles as table centerpieces.

Sixties music will set the mood for party guests. Hire an acoustic guitar musician to play songs from the era or spin Joan Baez, Sly & The Family Stone, Crosby Stills Nash & Young, and other period tunes. Arrange for flower children greeters to dance in carefree circles around the area. They can pass out single flowers to guests and share "peace" greetings. Have other hippies march around with "Happy Anniversary" protest signs. Paint flowers and peace signs on party guests' faces.

Have hippie-clad characters serve fruit smoothies from a flower-and-fruit-covered bar. Then grill ham and pineapple kabobs over flowerpot grills. Fill an eleven-inch high or higher flowerpot with dirt or gravel to within five inches of its top. Cover the dirt or gravel with aluminum foil and add a layer of charcoal. Then place a cooling rack or wire grill on top of the flowerpot and it's ready to grill. Now it's time for some flower child "make love not war" fun. Make daisy- or dandelion-necklace chains, toss Frisbees, and take in the groovy vibes.

Anniversary Gift Suggestions

European tradition tells us that a flower basket represents beauty in the home and a basket of fruit signifies a wish for plenty. Both are perfect, heartfelt fourth anniversary sentiments. Other fantastic floral and fruit anniversary gift suggestions include the following:

- Coffee table book of flower meanings or of flower photos
- One-year fruit-of-the-month or flower-of-the-month subscription
- Set of pretty floral bed sheets
- Basket of assorted fruit jams or jellies and homemade bread (Line the basket with a colorful kitchen towel and grape bunch accent.)
- His-and-her Fruit of the Loom underwear (great for partner-to-partner gift giving)
- Rose bush
- Bottle of fruity wine
- CD player with a collection of the couple's favorite CDs, or an "electric" gift basket (Electrical appliances are the modern fourth anniversary gift designation. Prepare a special gift basket filled with an electric toaster and a variety of fresh baked goods. Add ribbon-tied jars of jam and jelly. Or, fill the basket with an electric waffle iron, waffle cookbook, waffle mix, and a variety of fruit syrups.)

A Special Moment for the Anniversary Couple

A Flower for Every Hour of the Day

Send your spouse a flower for every hour of the day. Arrange for a florist to send a flower at 8:00 A.M., 9:00 A.M., 10:00 A.M., and so on throughout the day. You could also send a flower on the hour of the anniversary year (4:00 P.M. for the fourth anniversary). Enclose a love note with each flower stating your true love, as expressed through the flower's symbolized meaning. See the *Decorating Touches* section for a list of floral language.

Remember these floral language messages when presenting your spouse with a flower gift:

—Kissing a flower upon receipt means "Yes."

—A flower pinned over the heart upon receipt means "I love you."

—A flower worn in a woman's hair means "Take notice or caution."

—A bloom pinned in a woman's cleavage upon receipt means "I'll remember you fondly."

Tulips 'n' Juleps

Send your spouse a tulip with a note inviting him or her for a little southern romance. Fill your front porch with tulip blooms and two high-back rockers. Borrow wooden rocking chairs or purchase two just for the occasion. Sit back and sip the mint juleps and take in the fragrance of the beautiful tulips. In cooler weather, place your rockers inside and watch the romantic southern classic *Gone with the Wind*.

A Bed of Roses

Here's yet another just-for-two floral fantasy anniversary celebration. Surprise your spouse by covering your entire bed with thornless rose blooms and petals and serving him or her strawberries with whipped cream.

The Fifth Anniversary
—Wood—

Toast: May your love continue to grow and stand wood-strong!

"**K**nock on wood!" It's anniversary number five! This superstition dates back to the Native Americans and Greeks around 2000 B.C. Both believed their sky god lived in oak trees because these trees were frequently struck by lightning. The Native Americans felt that boasting—deliberately or inadvertently—about accomplishments, victories, or windfall harvests was sinister. So they established the custom of knocking at the base of an oak tree to contact the sky god for forgiveness.

This custom has evolved throughout the centuries in many different cultures. It can even be seen in the game of tag children play in which tree bases serve as safe havens. Today, we knock on wood for luck, mindful of its solid strength. We also recognize the wood-strength of a five-year marriage. Therefore, it's appropriate to celebrate this anniversary with wood-knocking expressions.

A *Tree*-mendous Lumberjack Breakfast

Trees produce the wood that symbolizes the solid relationship two people share in a five-year marriage. The tree's strength is planted firmly in the ground, and its beauty is reflected in its picturesque leaves and swaying branches. Like the tree, this anniversary celebration has *tree*-mendous qualities.

Invitation Ideas

Invite guests to attend this back-to-nature party by asking the question, "*Wood* you please come to a lumberjack breakfast in honor of Jamie and Bonnie's fifth anniversary? It's going to be a *tree*-mendous occasion!" Attach invitation details to one of these woodsy items:

- Small branch or twig
- Wooden nickel
- Wooden spoon
- Wooden clothespin
- Small, light piece of wood
- Piece of tree bark
- Small tree seedling
- Toy wooden block
- Tinkertoy or Lincoln Log toy piece
- Balsa wood airplane
- Tree seedling (Buy these from your local nursery or order a mailable tube version. See the *Supplier Resource Directory* at the end of this book.)
- Pine cone
- Bottle of Log Cabin maple syrup

Special Instructions for Guests

Wear a woodsy flannel shirt.

Decorating Touches

Create a woodland of love with these log cabin decorating inspirations:
- Create a family tree. Hang family and wedding photos on a tree's branches. This family tree can also be created year-round using an

artificial Christmas tree. Use photocopies or reprints to protect the original photos.

- Build a tree house.
- Create some log cabin coziness by lighting a fire in the fireplace and decorating the room with wool blankets.
- Cover a wooden picnic table with a red-and-black-checked flannel cloth.
- Use one of these wooden centerpiece ideas:
  —Large wooden bowl used as a planter for small evergreen tree seedlings
  —Small tree saplings placed in wooden containers
  —Pair of Dutch wooden shoes filled with evergreen tree seedlings
  —Multitiered arrangement of various-sized wooden blocks or small tree trunks supporting candles, placed on simple plates or in glass candle holders
  —Log cabin or other structure built with Lincoln Log toys or a wooden Tinkertoy arrangement (Or, put the pieces out and encourage guests to build their own.)
  —Wooden birdhouses (Add a woodpecker ornament if you can find one. Try a hardware store.)
  —Collection of wooden rolling pins standing up in a small wooden basket
  —Wooden duck decoys
  —Small bark-covered logs standing vertically on a table (Drill a hole in the top of each log to hold a votive or taper candle.)
  —Sliced logs laid flat on a table (Drill a hole in the top of each for a votive or taper candle.)
  —Twig vase filled with wildflowers (Glue straight twigs together vertically around a jar or bucket.)
  —Wooden bowls or baskets filled with pine cones

- Try these woodsy table accents:
  —Small tree seedlings (Wrap the base with brown craft paper and tie with a piece of raffia. Then trace a leaf onto colored paper to create novel place cards.)
  —Pine cones or colorful fall leaves scattered as table centerpiece accents
  —Individual napkins gathered with a wooden clothespin

—Place cards attached to a twig

—Place cards made by writing names on large green leaves with gold ink

—Place cards made by labeling Log Cabin maple syrup bottles

- Place wooden bowls filled with woodsy potpourri around the room.
- Use wooden barrels topped with flannel pillows as chairs around the table.
- Place another wooden barrel filled with firewood by the fireplace.
- Fill an old wooden wagon with decorative wool blankets.
- Decorate a log-cabin-type facility with ethereal splendor, draping flowing chiffon from the rafters and around wooden columns.
- Hang a sign painted on the side of a piece of rough wood that reads, "Have a woodsy fifth anniversary!"

Theme-Inspired Activities and Entertainment

Entertain guests with some *tree*-mendously fun wood happenings.

- Hold a tree-planting ceremony to commemorate the couple's fifth anniversary. Present the couple with a ribbon-tied shovel to dig the first scoop of dirt. Then toast them with champagne poured into small wooden bowls.
- Take a hike through the woods and collect interesting twigs, branches, and leaves along with nature's other treasures. Look for a mushroom. Finding a mushroom is considered very lucky and means good fortune is at hand. A pine cone would be a treasure, too. Pine cones are known to symbolize eternity. Because of their abundance in the forest, they have often been used as natural decorations.
- Make a wish while gazing at the treetops.
- Conduct a woodcutting contest.
- Conduct a woodchuck hunt. Hide a small furry toy in the woods or in the "log cabin" area.
- See who can build the tallest tower using toy building blocks.
- Play games with vintage wooden playing pieces such as dominoes, cribbage, jigsaw puzzles, or checkers.

- Invite a craft instructor to teach carving or whittling.
- Start a game of tree tag.
- Read aloud enchanted forest tales such as *Little Red Riding Hood, Hansel and Gretel, Paul Bunyan and His Big Blue Ox,* or *The Swiss Family Robinson.*
- Hold a hike-a-thon in the woods for charity.
- Gather guests together for a prearranged trip to a tree farm. Select and cut down a Christmas tree and bring it back for decorating. Decorate with popcorn garlands and birdseed ornaments to feed the birds and small local wildlife.
- Play a game of croquet using tree-branch mallets and small rubber balls.
- Hold a birling (log rolling) contest.
- Gather autumn leaves and press them into waxed-paper mementos.

Menu Ideas

Serve up a hearty breakfast for lumberjack appetites. This breakfast can also be served as a log cabin supper. Serve hungry guests heaping quantities from wooden cutting boards, bowls, plates, and trays.

- Lumberjack pancakes with Log Cabin maple syrup
- Eggs cooked to order
- Crisp bacon and maple-cured sausage patties
- Golden toasted bread "sticks" served with homemade fruit jams and preserves
- Freshly squeezed orange juice
- Hot cocoa and steaming black coffee cooked over an open fire
- Yule log anniversary cake (The Yule log, now a common tradition in many international Christmas celebrations, has its origin in the winter solstice celebration. The winter solstice marks the time of year when light returns to the Northern Hemisphere as the days grow longer again. The Yule log is a special log placed on the hearth where it glows for the twelve nights of the celebration. Then the log is kept in the house all year to protect the home and its inhabitants from illness and adverse conditions. The Yule log tradition has also evolved into an edible cake. Adopt this wonderful cake custom for a special wood anniversary celebration.)

Party Favors with Flair

Choose one of these *tree*-rific party favors:

- Redwood tree seedling (Buy these from your local nursery or order a mailable tube version. See the *Supplier Resource Directory* at the end of this book.)
- Small wooden trinket or jewelry box
- Bottle of Log Cabin syrup wrapped with a decorative bow
- Decorative painting on a small piece of driftwood, birch bark, or polished wood
- Bundle of wooden pencils wrapped with a decorative bow
- Wooden train whistle
- Bundle of kindling wrapped with a ribbon and a note that reads, "Wood-kindled love."
- Large Tootsie Roll candy tied with a ribbon

Love Under Construction

Love is still under construction in the early marriage years. Couples work together to build a strong and lasting relationship. Recruit volunteers (friends and family) to help construct a fun-loving fifth anniversary celebration. Together, you'll work to build a memory that'll last a lifetime.

Invite "Mr. and Mrs. Fixit" helpers by sending invitation details attached to a blueprint or a small, light block of wood. Other ideas include placing the invitation inside a brown paper lunch sack or writing details on a wood-handled paintbrush. Assign a party duty to each volunteer such as bringing a hot casserole, six-foot submarine sandwich, tossed green salad, soda pop, beer, bottle of wine, or bag of ice. Ask someone to pick up the anniversary cake from the bakery. Designate another shopper to buy paper plates, napkins, and cups. Tell guests to wear their work clothes—the grubbier the better—for this unique party.

Rope off the party area with yellow "hazard area" tape and orange caution cones. Hang "wet paint" signs on the front door and on painter's cloth-covered chairs. Set up buffets for the food using sawhorses and wooden ladders. Set two ladders facing each other about five feet apart. Then place a board, to be used as a buffet shelf, across each ladder's rungs. Lay a painter's cloth in the middle of the living room floor and over the dining room table. Place electric and hand saws in the center of the table as unusual centerpieces. Add a wooden tool box filled with hammers, screwdrivers, and other small tools. Provide a build-your-own-centerpiece activity by laying out Lincoln Log toys. Scatter empty paint cans filled with colorful decorative tissue or cloth around the room. Make luminaries out of some of the paint cans by punching holes in their sides and placing a candle inside. The luminaries can be painted on the outside with "Happy Anniversary" designs. Add vintage metal lunch boxes filled with sandwiches and apples. Also, set out hot coffee-filled Thermoses.

Now, it's time to greet each guest with a plastic hardhat and invite him or her into the "party zone" for some "hard working" anniversary fun. Play stimulating work tunes such as "Car Wash" and "YMCA." Show house-building movies such as *The Money Pit* and *Mr. Blandings Builds His Dream House*. This party could also be organized as a time to work together on a real home improvement project. Arrange this well ahead of time, of course. For instance, build a cedar hope chest for the anniversary couple to store future anniversary memories. You might also give the couple home improvement books as anniversary gifts.

Anniversary Gift Suggestions

Select one of these wonderful woodland gifts:

- His-and-her wooden pen sets
- Wooden birdhouse or bird feeder
- Painting on driftwood or birch bark
- Potted tree
- Wooden keepsake box
- Year's supply of firewood to keep the home fires burning
- Bentwood rocking chair or willow porch chair
- Cedar storage chest
- Golf woods
- Classic book of wood lore such as *Little Red Riding Hood, Hansel and Gretel, Paul Bunyan and His Big Blue Ox,* or *The Swiss Family Robinson*
- Two wooden walking sticks

- Wooden nutcracker and a gift box of unshelled nuts
- Set of silverware (Check to see if the couple ever received an entire set of silverware, the modern fifth anniversary gift selection. You could either add a place setting or start a new collection.)

A Special Moment for the Anniversary Couple

Forest Romance

Plan a romantic camping outing just for the two of you in the great outdoors. Carve your initials inside a heart shape into a tree (or just hang a wood-burned sign to symbolize your love). Cuddle up to a campfire and gaze at the treetops. This intimate, back-to-nature experience can also occur in your backyard or can be brought indoors. Pop a tent in front of your fireplace or camping lantern. Place potted evergreen trees around the room and take in their fragrant aroma as you share this special anniversary moment.

Over-the-Treetops Hot Air Balloon Ride

Here's another *tree*-mendous idea for the two of you. Soar over the treetops in a hot air balloon. Pack a champagne picnic breakfast and watch the sunrise.

Golf Woods Play

Gather up your golf woods and pair up for an afternoon golf game. Afterward, treat yourselves to a professional massage followed by a candlelight dinner for two.

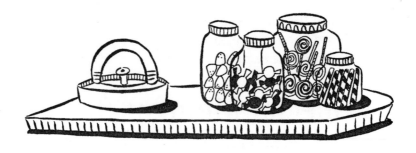

The Sixth Anniversary
—Candy and Iron—

Toast: May all your sweet dreams come true!

The sixth year of marriage is sweet, and candy has traditionally been the sixth anniversary symbol. In earlier days, iron also symbolized the anniversary, with iron horseshoes as the predominate emblem signifying good luck in the marriage. Both themes give sweet inspiration to these sixth anniversary confections.

Sweet Dreams Slumber Party

This anniversary party is full of delectable sweet-tooth delights. There's an old-fashioned saying: "Too many kisses spoil the cook." However, this celebration ignores that advice and cooks up a dish with a new twist—unrelentingly sweet affection!

Invitation Ideas

Invite guests to a "Sweet Dreams Slumber Party" with one of these sugary candy inspirations:

- A small box of chocolates wrapped with a beautiful satin bow
- A decorative tin filled with candy taffy or homemade fudge

- Sugary gumdrops in a small cellophane bag tied with a decorative satin ribbon
- A candy bar tied with a pretty ribbon
- A box of chocolates with Forrest Gump's phrase "Life is like a box of chocolates" attached
- A tulip-shaped champagne glass filled with Hershey's Kisses
- Individual-sized boxes of candy-coated cereals such as Fruit Loops, Sugar Pops, and Cocoa Puffs (Include a plastic bowl and spoon.)
- A small, ribbon-wrapped, heart-shaped wreath covered with candy conversation hearts
- A toy horseshoe covered with small, glued-on gumdrop candies

Special Instructions for Guests

Invite guests to wear their pajamas and bring their most comfortable bed pillow for an all-night, candy-a-holic movie marathon. Select from titles such as *Sweet Dreams*, *Forrest Gump*, *Candy Mountain*, *The Sugarland Express*, *The Chocolate War*, *Willy Wonka and the Chocolate Factory*, and so on.

Also, enclose a dream-journal page with each invitation. Ask guests to write a dream wish for the guests of honor. Collect the pages at the party and bind them with delicate ribbon to create a sweet dreams memento for the anniversary couple.

Decorating Touches

Decorate the kitchen area with sugarplum fancy.

- Cover the kitchen or dining table with a bedspread or designer sheets and a blanket. A celestial design provides that added sleepy-time flair. Make up the table to resemble a bed by adding pillows to one end of the table. You might even add a teddy bear as a nighttime accent. Place candy shop treats directly on this novel "sweet dreams" table.
- To add a nostalgic iron touch, fill cast iron skillets with candied treats such as caramel popcorn. Traditionally, Grandma's iron frying pan was commonly wrapped up, tied with a ribbon, and given as a wedding gift. Couples who had not yet lived away from their parents appreciated such basic household items as valued gifts.

- Fill cast iron corn muffin pans with a variety of candies such as M&M's, sugar gumdrops, Gummi bears, and Sweet Tarts. These treats are perfect for movie watching or just plain sweet conversation.
- Place homey living room and bedroom table lamps, their bulbs turned down low, in the kitchen or dining room next to the table "bed." Add soothing candlelight to complete the dreamy ambiance.
- Iron away washday blues by unfolding an ironing board at one end of the kitchen. Place an antique cook-stove iron on it (you could also use a modern electrical version). Then set up cocktail service on this unusual bar.
- Fill the room with candy dishes, candy jars, and old-fashioned apothecary jars brimming with an assortment of colorful candies.
- Make a candy-stick flower vase. Glue colorful hard-candy sticks to the outside of a large can. Tie the can with a pretty ribbon and fill it with a bouquet of colorful flowers.
- Grow a candy flowerpot centerpiece. Attach a candy flower bloom to a sturdy artificial flower stem and poke it into a florist's block-filled clay pot. Make the candy flower bloom by gluing an oversized silk flower on the center of a Styrofoam circle. Then glue snack-sized candy bars, stretching outward, and wrapped hard candies around the edge of the circle. Conceal the back and edge of the circle with color-coordinated tissue paper. Match the flower creation's color with the candies' colors. For instance, combine a large gold sunflower bloom with the gold color of snack-sized Butterfinger candy bars and cellophane-wrapped butterscotch candies. Next, cover the base of the flowerpot with decorative green craft grass. To pick up the royal blue candy bar lettering, surround the base of the flower stem with royal blue tissue paper. To complete the candy flower picture, add full-sized Butterfinger candy bar accents. Attach florist's picks to the candy bars and poke them at vertical angles into the flowerpot arrangement. Then, for a delightful finishing touch, tie a raffia or neutral-colored crinkle-paper bow on the stem, just below the flower bloom.

Theme-Inspired Activities and Entertainment

Sprinkle a little sugar fun and entertainment on guests.
- Greet guests at the door with a pair of comfy bedroom slippers.

- Invite guests into the kitchen for some candy-making fun. In Grandma's day, the sixth anniversary was often celebrated with a taffy pull. Get out an old cookbook and roll and stretch away. You could also make flavored candy fudge or candied popcorn balls. Make some old-time sugared corn (popcorn roasted and sprinkled with sugar) in Grandma's old iron kettle.

- Sneak outdoors for some pajama-clad, moonlit iron horseshoe tossing.

- Show a movie-a-thon of sugary movie selections. (See the *Special Instructions for Guests* section for ideas.)

- Compile and present the dream journal mentioned in the *Special Instructions for Guests* section to the anniversary couple. Read the sweet dream wishes aloud.

- Encourage party guests to share "sweet nothings" with the objects of their affections and to mingle among the crowd with "dandy candy" conversation.

Menu Ideas

The party menu consists of (what else!) candy delights for this sweet dream celebration. But, just to make sure that guests don't overdose on sugar, provide a balance of sugar-free selections. Include a fresh vegetable tray, a cheese and fruit display, and a selection of turkey, ham, and veggie sandwiches. Display these alongside candy-shop confections and accompaniments.

- Include the candy treats cooked up by slumber party guests and displayed in cast iron skillets and muffin pans. (See the *Decorating Touches* section for ideas.)

- Offer candy martini cocktails from the ironing board bar including Tootsie Roll martinis, chocolate kiss martinis, and Butterfinger martinis. You could also offer a special slumber party drink—a "wake-up call" martini.

- Heat some water in an iron kettle and offer a selection of herbal teas.

- Serve cookies and milk. For an added sweet dreams touch, heat milk on the stove and offer mugs of warm milk or hot chocolate.

- Greet slumber party guests in the morning (or late, late evening) with eggs, bacon, and orange juice. Don't forget candy-coated cereal and milk. Offer Fruit Loops, Sugar Pops, and Cocoa Puffs.

Party Favors with Flair

Send guests home with a special candy memento:

- Small box of chocolates wrapped with a beautiful satin bow
- Decorative tin full of candy taffy or homemade fudge
- Sugary gumdrops in a small cellophane bag tied with a decorative satin ribbon
- Candy bar tied with a pretty ribbon
- Box of chocolates with Forrest Gump's phrase "Life is like a box of chocolates" attached
- Tulip-shaped champagne glass filled with Hershey's Kisses
- Individual-sized boxes of candy-coated cereals such as Fruit Loops, Sugar Pops, and Cocoa Puffs
- Decorative tin or gift bag filled with the candied popcorn, fudge, or taffy made by party guests
- Bedroom slippers given to guests upon arrival
- Fragrant sleep pillow filled with lavender, cinnamon, and chamomile (Attach the sentiment "Sweet Dreams!")
- Dream journal
- Sugarplum ornaments (Glue sugary gumdrops and orange-slice candies to a Styrofoam ball. Attach a velvet ribbon for hanging.)

Prisoners of Love

Invite guests to a "Prisoners of Love" anniversary party. Shackled together by love, the anniversary couple will be breakin' out with some jailhouse-rockin' fun. Invite guests to this criminally fun party by sneaking them a metal nail file hidden in an empty Valentine's Day chocolates' box. Choose a large, heart-shaped box elaborately decorated with ribbon and lace. Ask guests to wear prison-issued clothing only (black and white is appropriate). The couple could greet guests wearing rented, black-and-white-striped prison costumes. During this greeting time, they could also shackle themselves together with toy metal handcuffs. At the party's entrance, hang long black streamers three inches apart from the ceiling to the floor to resemble prison bars. Then invite guests to "break into" this dance party behind bars.

Create a cellblock ambiance. Place a sign by the phone reading, "Inmates must limit phone calls to five minutes." Rock the "jailhouse" with tunes such as "Jailhouse Rock," "Chain Gang," or "Prisoner of Love." Allow "yard walks" only if necessary. Order prisoners to stand in a "lineup" for instant camera shots. Also, take individual mug shots of each party guest. Don't forget to get his or her fingerprints on the party favor memento. Serve pieces of anniversary cake cut with a long metal file. Then tip champagne-filled metal cups to the anniversary couple with this sixth anniversary toast: "To Steve and Karen, Prisoners of Love." (Hint: Purchase tin cups at camping supplier or army surplus stores.)

Anniversary Gift Suggestions

Wish the anniversary couple sweet dreams with a gift basket filled with any of the sweet items listed below. They're also a perfectly sweet idea for personal gift giving between the couple.

- Set of designer sheets
- New pair of sweet dream pillows
- New electric iron (the kind that shuts off automatically)
- Variety of VCR movie tapes, DVD disks, or a gift certificate for movie rentals
- Candy cookbook
- Candy dish
- Iron horseshoes toss game
- Wrought iron candle holders
- Pair of antique cook-stove irons to be used as bookends
- Wrought iron patio set
- Wrought iron sundial lawn ornament
- Wrought iron rooster weathervane
- Wooden keepsake box or other wooden item (Wood is the modern sixth anniversary gift selection. It's also the traditional fifth anniversary gift. Return to "The Fifth Anniversary: Wood" chapter for more wood-inspired gift ideas.)

A Special Moment for the Anniversary Couple

A Sweet Day at the Horse Races

It's a romantic day at the horse races for the anniversary couple. Invite your spouse to a "sure bet" celebration day. Tie a note with a big fancy ribbon to an iron horseshoe. Remember to display the horseshoe with the points upward, lest the good luck drain out. Sneak away for the day, just the two of you, to the race track. Place your bets on horses with sweet and iron-clad names such as "Sugar Mae" or "Hercules." It's sure to be a winning anniversary experience!

The Seventh Anniversary
—Wool and Copper—

*Toast: Here's to surrounding yourselves
in the woolly warmth of each other's love!*

Wool and copper are both associated with the seventh wedding anniversary. Wool is commonly used to keep warm, and copper is a conduit of heat. These wool and copper anniversary party ideas are easy to cozy up to, making the seventh-anniversary couple feel warm and fuzzy inside.

Wool 'n' Copper Capers

Like pennies falling from heaven, this party theme rains woolly fun and copper penny capers.

Invitation Ideas

Send a note to guests along with one of these wool or copper accents:

- Hand-delivered jar containing shiny copper pennies, decorated with a woolen ribbon
- Mitten filled with a few copper pennies (Tie the wrist of the mitten closed with a yarn bow, attaching an invitation message.)
- Ball of yarn

- Pinked-edged square of wool
- Copper-colored Christmas tree bulb
- Copper penny glued to a playing card with a note reading, "Join us for penny-ante poker fun!"
- Post card or note card featuring an English "copper" or bobby

Special Instructions for Guests

Put on your woollies and come over for an evening of copper capers!

Decorating Touches

Put some warm wool and shiny copper touches on the party place.

- Build a copper-bright fire in the fireplace.
- Drape a wool scarf-and-mitten garland around the room. Tie together various colors and designs of wool scarves. Attach wool mittens with wooden clothespins at the knotted areas.
- Cover the table with a decorative wool stadium blanket.
- Slip a long-sleeved wool sweater over the back of each table chair. (Check your local thrift shop for inexpensive choices.)
- Place a wool mitten at each place setting. Fill the mitten with a setting of silverware and a wool napkin.
- Write the name of each guest on a place card. Then slip the place card into the folded-up rim of a knit cap. Place a cap at each place setting as a novel place card holder.
- Fill a copper teakettle or bowl with balls of colorful yarn. Poke two knitting needles into the yarn. Then scatter copper pennies around the base of this centerpiece.
- Add copper plant containers around the room.
- Decorate a live or artificial Christmas tree at any time of the year with wool and copper decorations. Make a tree garland by gluing copper pennies to a string of yarn. Then hang copper-colored Christmas tree bulbs on the tree. Attach mittens here and there using wooden clothespins.
- Fill an antique copper wash boiler with wool stadium blankets. Guests can use these to cover themselves while curling up in front of the fireplace.

Theme-Inspired Activities and Entertainment

Entertain guests with warm, woolly adventures and copper capers.

- Organize some copper penny arcade fun. Each activity costs the guests a penny. Set up a different game or activity at tables or areas around the room. Invite guests to rotate from one penny game to another.

  —Lucky Seven copper-penny-ante poker

  —Copper penny bingo

  —Copper penny checkers (heads against tails)

  —Copper penny tossing games (Toss pennies into copper pans to earn points.)

  —Copperhead snake or copper butterfly hunt (Glue a penny to the top of a toy snake or on butterfly decorations. Then hide the copper creature for the hunt.)

  —Penny-wise copper penny jar guess (Fill a clear jar with pennies and take turns guessing the number of pennies in the jar. The winner gets to keep the jar—and the pennies.)

  —Moonlight copper penny hunt

- Watch copper capers (*Keystone Comedies* silent movies).

- Instruct the guests of honor to follow various yarn-string trails leading to different locations around the house, each string ending at a gift for the anniversary couple.

- Try this fun dinner preparation idea. Have guests cook part of their dinner in the fireplace. Roll individual servings of eye-of-round roast in cracked pepper and coarse salt. Wrap each serving in four layers of aluminum foil. Then cook for individual preference, placing the wrapped meat directly on the flaming and embered logs for twenty to thirty minutes (medium-rare meat).

- Later in the night, cuddle up for warm conversation and marshmallow roasting. Snuggle around the fire wrapped in wool blankets. Make fireplace s'mores (sandwich a Hershey milk chocolate candy bar piece and a roasted marshmallow between two graham cracker squares).

- Roast chestnuts or pop popcorn in the fireplace.

- Fry donuts and wrap them in wool squares as take-home favors.

Menu Ideas

Create a menu using one or more of these tummy-warming menu items:

- Lamb chops or mutton pie
- Cozy chili and cornbread
- Baked apples filled with raisins, maple syrup, cinnamon, and pecans
- Coffee, hot herbal teas, or hot chocolate served in copper mugs
- Gingerbread mitten cookies
- Fireplace-cooked eye-of-round roast (See *Theme-Inspired Activities and Entertainment* section above.)
- Roasted chestnuts or popcorn cooked in the fireplace
- Fireplace s'mores, a Girl Scout treat so delicious it prompts "some more" (See *Theme-Inspired Activities and Entertainment* section above.)

Party Favors with Flair

Create the perfect, cozy party memento.

- Mason jar filled with shiny copper pennies and tied with a wool cloth ribbon
- Mitten filled with a few copper pennies (Tie a "Thank You" message around the wrist with a wool yarn bow.)
- Copper-colored Christmas tree bulb
- Knit cap (See the Decorating Touches section above.)
- Pair of mittens
- Wool or knit scarf
- Lamb or sheep beanbag animal
- Handmade wool-felted mittens (Shrink wool sweater material by washing it on the hot cycle three or four times and throwing it in a hot dryer until the material shrinks and feels feltlike. Next, cut out two sides for each hand using a template made by tracing a variety of hand sizes. Finally, sew mitten sides together—right sides out—with a contrasting color of yarn using a blanket stitch.)
- Homemade donuts wrapped in wool squares (See *Theme-Inspired Activities and Entertainment* section above.)

Victorian Ice Skating Party

Victorians loved ice skating parties and so will your guests. Bundle up in warm, woolly clothes and plan an enchanting Victorian experience. Invite guests by handwriting notes with calligraphic penmanship. Write on delicate personal stationery or on small cards reminiscent of the Victorian calling card. Place the note inside a pair of wool mittens or wrapped in a wool scarf.

Hold this anniversary skating party at a public frozen pond or lake. You can also create a rink by flooding a section of your backyard with a garden hose. Hire a tanker truck company or the fire department to flood an empty lot or parking lot area. The flooding may work freeform in some places, or you can outline an area using stakes, boards, and sturdy plastic sheeting. If the anniversary is not in the winter months or if your climate is not right for freezing such a rink, hold the skating party at a local indoor ice rink.

Set up a portable shelter and stove for heating Victorian beverage treats. Warm guests with mulled cider, hot buttered rum, or hot chocolate covered with whipped cream and chocolate shavings. Serve these beverages in Victorian china teacups with saucers or use copper mugs. Share the following Victorian favorites at this outdoor winter dessert party: nut fudge, popcorn balled with hot taffy, and warm gingerbread man cookies. For additional warmth, gather round a bonfire and roast hot dogs and chestnuts. Play Victorian waltz music over the ice. Hold a donut-on-a-string eating contest and play musical chairs on the ice. Wrap rubber around the feet of the chairs and have a gentleman or gentlewoman at each chair to hold it steady during the musical procession.

Anniversary Gift Suggestions

Select a gift of woolly or copper warmth.
- Copper teakettle
- His-and-her wool sweaters or wool shirts
- Copper movie (*Keystone Comedies*)
- Copper or metal fireplace chestnut roaster (See the *Supplier Resource Directory.*)
- Metal fireplace popcorn roaster

- Matching wool or knit scarf, hat, and mitten sets for the anniversary couple
- Wool stadium blanket
- Set of copper-colored Christmas tree bulbs
- Set of copper kitchen pans
- Antique copper wash boiler
- Coppersmith art piece
- His-and-her desk sets or the 1957 movie *Desk Set* with Spencer Tracy and Katharine Hepburn (Desk sets are commonly listed as the modern seventh anniversary gift choice for the anniversary couple—also a "perfect set.")

A Special Moment for the Anniversary Couple

"Seven-Year-Itch" Escape

Wool can be itchy sometimes. Escape the seven-year-itch syndrome with a romantic hideaway weekend. Plan a ski weekend at a cozy mountain retreat. After a brisk day on the slopes, cuddle up together in the woolly warmth of your love.

A Copper Beach Sunset

Prefer the tropics over a winter wonderland? Plan a trip to a warm tropical beach. Bask in the romance of a copper-beach sunset.

The Eighth Anniversary
—Bronze—

Toast: May your love be forever bronzed
as a lasting keepsake memory!

Eight years of marriage deserves a bronze medal of love. The couple should be praised for their perseverance through good times and bad, and their bond should be commemorated with a winning eighth anniversary celebration.

Bronze and Beethoven

Bronze is an alloy of two metals, copper and tin. The union of the two makes a stunning metal, just as the union of two lives makes a beautiful marriage. Mark this wedding anniversary with a romantic melding —the exquisite blending of bronze and Beethoven.

Invitation Ideas

Create a classical setting with one of these musical notes.

- Write invitation details with a bronze-ink pen on the stanzas of blank sheet music, titling the occasion "Bronze and Beethoven."
- Enclose an engraved invitation encased in a bronze-polished frame.

- Enclose an invitation note inside—or place an invitation label on—the cover of a Beethoven cassette or CD. Or, make a "Bronze and Beethoven" label, cut to fit inside the plastic cover.
- Paste a "Bronze and Beethoven" label on the outside of a bronzing or tanning lotion bottle, with the words "Ingredients" or "Directions."
- Include a bronze medal along with a formally printed invitation.
- Write invitation details on the back of a post card or inside a note card that pictures Beethoven, a piano, or a classical-music-themed design.
- Send an engraved invitation along with a bronze-painted, piano-shaped tree ornament.

Special Instructions for Guests

Bring an inexpensive item, such as an old shoe or old book, to bronze at the party. You'll immortalize it for the anniversary couple in a special bronzing ceremony.

Decorating Touches

Decorate with bold bronze accents. (Note: Decoration items can be bronzed by painting them with a metallic bronze spray paint.)

- Place a bronzed bust of Beethoven centerpiece on top of a table decorated with a white satin square layered over a stark black, floor-length satin tablecloth.
- Add tall, bronzed candelabra that hold tall, white candle tapers.
- Set a formal table with fine china and crystal.
- Scatter bronzed leaves across the tabletop. You can bronze leaves by covering actual leaves with metallic foiling or paint. Or, trim window screen into leaf shapes using a leaf as a pattern. Then spray-paint the screen leaves bronze and trim them with a bronze paint pen.
- Make elegant bronze-wrapped napkin rings. Form each napkin ring by wrapping and crisscrossing strings of sixteen-gauge brass and eighteen-gauge copper wire around an empty paper-towel tube. To cut, pinch the ends of the wire string with pliers. Slip completed rings over two napkins, one black and one white, layered and rolled together.

- Place a single red or ivory rose in a small bronzed vase at each place setting. The rose can also be bronzed.
- Frame each guest's name in a small bronzed photo frame and use it as a polished place card statement.
- Write the dinner menu on the stanzas of blank sheet music and place the "musical piece" in a bronze or black pocketless folder. Title it with the name of one of Beethoven's creations such as his third symphony *(Eroica)*. Present this musical piece to each guest as he or she is seated. Consider displaying the menu on a music stand placed near the table.
- If possible, include a magnificent baby grand piano in the room décor. Top it with another bronzed Beethoven bust and elegant candelabrum.
- Employ the utmost formal style at dinner with wait staff dressed in tuxedos and white gloves.

Theme-Inspired Activities and Entertainment

Envelop guests in the passion of Beethoven's music by entertaining with concertos by candlelight. Play recordings of Beethoven piano sonatas, concertos, string quartets, and symphonies. Include the bold and dynamic opening of his fifth symphony and play his ninth symphony, one of the great achievements of European music.

- In addition to famous Beethoven recordings, hire a professional pianist to entertain with other Beethoven classics.
- Beethoven aspired to be a member of genteel society. Stage a ball for waltzing and indulging in aristocratic luxury. According to historians, Beethoven refused to play what he considered to be old-fashioned music (like Mozart). Also, he most likely wore German-influenced formalwear. However, adopt the approach made popular at present-day Beethoven birthday balls in which a mixture of Beethoven and Mozart is played. Guests wear costumes influenced more by French than German high society. These include Marie Antoinette era costumes (wide-hipped and wide-hooped polonaise gowns) for women, elaborately ruffled shirts for men, high-heeled shoes for both, rouged cheeks, and outrageously stacked powdered wigs.

- Conduct a bronzing ceremony using the items requested in the *Special Instructions for Guests* section. Ceremoniously parade the articles outside and lay them on the lawn or picnic table, covered with a special cloth for the bronzing process. Start the ceremony by toasting the anniversary couple with champagne poured into bronze-stemmed goblets. (Note: Paint the stems of plastic champagne glasses well before the party. For safety's sake, remember to paint the stems only.) Then begin the bronzing process by spray-painting the gift items brought by guests with metallic-bronze-colored paint. Make a declaration of bronze proportion and present the astonishing array of bronzed gifts to the anniversary couple.

Menu Ideas

Keep in tune with the German-born maestro's great desire to be a member of "upper crust" society. Prepare a savory symphony of high-society proportion.

- Bold Beethoven "bites"—exquisitely arranged canapés and hors d'oeuvres arranged on novel serving trays (elaborate bronze photo frames) and offered with white-gloved service
- Bouillabaisse soup, a potpourri of seafood soup
- Chateaubriand
- A vegetable melody of asparagus and hollandaise sauce
- *Moonlight Sonata* salad
- Grand Finale German chocolate cake
- The crescendo and symphonic splendor of after-dinner flaming liqueurs and coffees

Party Favors with Flair

Present guests with a "standing ovation" memento of the occasion.

- Beethoven cassette or CD wrapped in a striking bronze-colored gift bag
- Bronzed leaf from the dinner table décor
- Bronzed rose vase described in the *Decorating Touches* section
- Bottle of fine German wine tied with luminescent bronze-colored ribbon or placed in a bronze-colored velvet or satin wine bag

Crazy Eight in Love

Throw a party that celebrates the couple's crazy-in-love eight years of marriage with some crazy-eight party ideas. Invite eight couples to an eight-course dinner using a crazy-eight playing card or eight-ball message. Glue the note to a billiard-table eight ball or a commercial replica. (See the *Supplier Resource Directory* in the back.) For the eight-course dinner, serve six traditional courses including soup, fish, main course, salad, dessert, and fruit. Add hors d'oeuvres before dinner and coffee and liqueurs after to make a total of eight courses. You'll need to arrange for help in the kitchen and a wait staff to serve the meal. Costume the wait staff in crazy-eight, Mad Hatter garb, giving them a stack of eight hats to wear.

Serve the courses in crazy-eight fashion. Print a menu with numbers one through eight, in which the numbers correspond to courses (number "1" for hors d'oeuvres, "2" for soup, "3" for fish, and so on). Then place the following hands of playing cards at each place setting: an ace serving as the number "1," numbers "2" through "7," and two crazy "8" cards. Instruct each guest to hold up his or her cards, with card backs facing out, to the person to his or her left. This person then draws a card randomly. The card drawn determines the course that he or she will be served; so everyone will be eating in a crazy, out-of-order fashion. For example, drawing number "3" means the guest will be served the third course, fish. If a guest draws a crazy-eight card, he or she may choose the eighth course, dessert, or another selection. This is the only number that allows the cardholder to choose a number different from the one drawn. Each person holds an extra crazy-eight card, giving him or her the opportunity to call for another selection or choose the number "8" course, dessert. Each selected card should be immediately discarded to avoid having the same course served again. Follow this service procedure for each course of the meal, waiting until everyone has finished his or her current course before taking orders for the next.

Decorate the party area with crazy-eight style. Stack eight plates, each a different color, at each place setting. Serve each course on the top plate, removing the used plate after a finished course. When a guest orders a number "2" (soup), substitute a bowl for the top plate. For crazy-eight place cards, stack eight small gift boxes, one on top of the other, at each place setting. Tie the top box with a ribbon, writing the name of the guest on the ribbon tail. Fill each box beforehand with a different crazy-eight party favor: Box One–eight Hershey's Kisses; Box Two–eight Hershey's Hugs; Box Three–deck of crazy-eight playing cards; Box Four–eight lines of poetry; Box Five–eight flower petals; Box Six–eight lines from a love song; Box Seven–eight pieces of a jigsaw puzzle; Box Eight–eight pieces of confetti for throwing wishes at the anniversary couple. After dinner, invite guests to get behind the billiard-table eight ball for some billiards or pool game fun.

Anniversary Gift Suggestions

Select one of these bronze and maestro inspirations:

- Tickets to the symphony featuring Beethoven classics
- Season tickets to the symphony
- Bronze-colored metal photo frames
- Collection of Beethoven music cassettes or CDs
- Beethoven coffee table book
- Bronze vase
- Set of bronze candlesticks
- Small bronze sculpture
- Identical linen shirts, an Irish linen tablecloth, a Native American piece of pottery, or a lace tablecloth (The modern eighth anniversary designations are linen and lace. Also, pottery is sometimes listed as the traditional eighth anniversary choice. Refer to "The Ninth Anniversary: Pottery and Willow" chapter and "The Thirteenth Anniversary: Lace" chapter for more gift ideas.)

A Special Moment for the Anniversary Couple

Moonlight Sonata

Enjoy a moonlight sonata for two. Dance together under the moonlight to the beautiful and sublime music of Beethoven's *Moonlight Sonata,* which was written to woo a countess. Its tranquil first movement has been described as moonlight shining on waves of water.

The Ninth Anniversary
—Pottery and Willow—

*Toast: May your marriage be formed
with the art and craft of the potter.*

The ninth wedding anniversary is associated with exquisite pottery. The potter starts with a simple lump of clay and then skillfully shapes it on a potter's wheel. The still-malleable clay is then fired into a fragile yet enduring piece of art. This process mirrors the skillful construction of another treasured piece of art—a loving relationship. With care, a couple can shape their two lives into one solid relationship.

The willow, with its small, furry pod blooms, is also associated with the ninth wedding anniversary. It stands tall and sways with graceful and pliant movements, as does willowy love.

Anniversary Potluck

Surround guests with a *pot*pourri of pottery expression: decorative pottery, kitchen pots, and flowerpots. Host a potluck party that offers food, fun, surprise eats, and good fortune.

Invitation Ideas

Invite guests with *pot*luck flair:

- Send a scratch-and-win Lotto card inside an invitation card.
- Attach an invitation to a potted plant or flower and leave one on each invited guest's doorstep just before dawn.
- Place an engraved invitation inside a vintage aluminum or enamelware kitchen pot. Add a pair of lucky dice.
- Place a rolled-up invitation inside a small clay pot tied with a pretty ribbon. If you like, sponge-paint the outside of the pot with decorative detail.
- Send a potluck photocopy creation. Copy a photo and essential party information onto 8½-by-11-inch paper. Fold twice into an invitation shape. Choose an old family photo showing a church potluck or the family gathered around the dinner table. You might also stage a potluck photo session. Adorn the anniversary couple in vintage kitchen aprons. Have them hold a kitchen pot adorned with a "potluck" sign. For a more comical approach, have them wear kitchen pots as hats and hold a "You're invited to a potluck" sign. Recruit helpers (kids and kids-at-heart) to color the invitations with crayons.

Special Instructions for Guests

Invite each guest to bring a potluck dish to share. Take your chances with true potluck daring! There may be an overabundance of Jell-O dishes and no main dish in sight. Don't worry. You can always order pizza.

You might finesse the potluck a bit by assigning food categories using the initials of guests' last names. For example, ask guests with initials A–G to bring a salad or vegetable dish, G–M a main dish, and N–Z a dessert. Look at the guest list carefully in case there's a large number of guests who share the same last initial. You could also go with first name initials. Here's another fun initial assignment activity: Ask friends and family to bring a recipe beginning with the same letter as their first or last name. Uncle Charlie might bring his famous chocolatey rich double-layer cake. The Miller family may choose a marvelous meat loaf recipe. It's also fun to share recipes, so ask guests to bring the recipes for their potluck dishes.

Decorating Touches

Decorate for a homey country atmosphere with a potpourri of pottery, kitchen pots, and willow accents.

- Cover tables with charming patchwork quilts such as a crazy quilt or a wedding-ring-pattern quilt. Another nostalgic choice is a vintage kitchen tablecloth. Shop local secondhand or thrift stores for a wide variety of designs at bargain prices. Of course, just about any table design will fit in with the potluck theme.

- Set the table with one of these unique china "pattern" plates:
  —Clay flowerpot saucers lined with colorful paper plates or lace doilies
  —Stoneware dishes
  —China with a blue "willow" design
  —A medium-sized willow basket lined with a paper plate

- Use clay flowerpots filled with flowering plants such as geraniums and African violets as centerpieces for the tables. A cookie pot centerpiece is also cute. Place cookie flowers-on-a-stick into a flowerpot or cooking pot planted with wheat grass.

- Use empty clay flowerpots to hold utensils, napkins, dinner rolls, and so on. Decorate the flowerpots by laying delicate lace doilies over their rims and wrapping the pots with pretty ribbon. Be sure to line them with clear plastic wrap or colorful tissue when filling with edible items.

- Use vintage aluminum or enamelware pots to hold utensils, napkins, and dinner rolls.

- Place pots of food directly on the table, protecting its surface with decorative potholders.

- Make a willow flower vase by gluing or wiring straight willow twigs to a large can or vase. Conceal wiring by tying a ribbon around it. A ribbon-tied bunch of willow branches placed in a pottery vase also makes a willowy statement.

- For willowy accents, form willows into napkin rings by soaking and wrapping branch pieces around a paper-towel tube. You can also slip a willow twig into your own napkin rings. Tie a place card to a willow twig or adorn the place card with a tiny piece of willow.

- Add small flowerpot napkin rings and candles as described in the *Anniversary Fiesta* section later in this chapter.

- Place the anniversary cake on a potter's wheel for a spectacular presentation.
- Make ice cream flowerpot centerpieces. Fill plastic-wrap-lined flowerpots with a gallon of ice cream. Cylindrical ice cream containers can also be decorated with florist's paper and ribbon bows to resemble flowerpots. Cover the top of the ice cream with cookie-crumb "dirt," made from Oreo cookie crumbs (dark sides only). Then put an artificial flower-bush stem into the center of the pot and half bury Gummi worms in the "dirt," leaving their tails poking out.

Theme-Inspired Activities and Entertainment

Entertain guests with some potluck fun.

- Watch the movie *Ghost*, starring Demi Moore, with its romantic pottery-spinning scene.
- Play games of chance—roulette, dice, draw poker, and bingo—and have door-prize drawings.
- Conduct a "potshot" toss tournament. Toss playing cards, Ping-Pong balls, or bean bags into kitchen pots placed as strategic targets. Increase the playing handicap by asking players to stand backward and toss the playing pieces over their shoulders toward the targets.
- Conduct a potato sack race around a "pothole" obstacle course, using kitchen pots as potholes around the yard.
- Plant flower seeds or flowers in flowerpots as party favors or as decorations for the couple's patio.
- Bring in a pottery instructor with a potter's wheel and supplies to present a pottery how-to session. Offer guests a chance to try the craft.

Menu Ideas

Invite guests to bring potluck fare as described in the *Special Instructions for Guests* section. In addition, consider these menu ideas:

- Deep-dish chicken, beef, and vegetable potpies
- Old-fashioned pot roast with fresh garden potatoes, carrots, and onions
- Sweet potato pie and potato pancakes

- Bread baked in flowerpots
- Casserole recipes baked in clay baking pans and bowls
- Pizza baked on clay baking boards
- Flowerpot-grilled kabobs (See the "how-to" described in the "Flower Child Meadow Party" in the fourth anniversary chapter.)
- Ice cream flowerpots described in the *Decorating Touches* section above
- Homemade lemonade served from an enamelware pot

Party Favors with Flair

Guests love to take a little bit of the party fun home with them. Pick one of these ideas:

- Lucky chance grab bags or, as the English call it, a "lucky dip" (Hide a variety of party favors in sealed gift bags and ask each guest to make a selection. Try this flowerpot twist. Ask guests to close their eyes as they reach into a very large flowerpot or pottery vase to grab a party favor.)
- Decorative pot holders
- Small, ribbon-wrapped flowerpot filled with a planted flower, a packet of flower seeds, potpourri, or candy (Try filling it with colorful, flavored licorice sticks.)
- Small pottery vase or piece of decorative pottery
- Small pottery dish holding a candle
- Homemade cookbook filled with the guests' potluck recipes

Anniversary Fiesta

Mexico is rich with beautiful pottery and terra cotta art. Borrow some south-of-the-border style for this special anniversary fiesta. Commemorate nine years of happy marriage with a lively and colorful celebration. Hang strings of colored lights, drape color-striped serapes on walls and patio fences, and cluster hot salsa-colored paper flowers and piñatas around the room. Set several large leafy plants in terra cotta pots around the area. Add a few tall potted cactus plants wrapped with twinkle lights to this lush setting. The twinkle sensations can also be made with wire cactus structures. Line walkways with pottery luminarias glowing with candlelight.

Cover tables with brightly colored tablecloths topped with striped serapes. For centerpieces, make an arrangement with cacti in clay pots. Accent this centerpiece with clay pot candles. Fill small clay flowerpots with melted wax and a candlewick, first covering the drainage hole with aluminum foil. Place votive candles on clay flowerpot saucers.

Another centerpiece idea is to place green and red chilies or large colorful paper flowers in decorated Mexican pots. Continue this table pottery theme using small clay flowerpots as novel napkin holders. Drill a one-inch hole in the bottom of a small clay flowerpot, draping the napkin through the open top of the pot and down through the hole. Place dried or plastic chilies as an accent inside the flowerpot.

Invite guests to this pottery fiesta by writing details on a small terra cotta plant pot. A printed invitation can also be sent inside the pot. Another unique notion is to print or glue invitation details on a flour tortilla.

Entertain guests with a mariachi band and a Mexican "flowerpot" hat dance. Dance around a flowerpot. Hang and break one of the piñatas. Offer a fajitas-and-taco bar where guests top off southwestern favorites with fixings of their choice, placing their selections on lined flowerpot saucer plates. Bake an anniversary cake in a well-greased and floured clay flowerpot. Serve it with powdered sugar Mexican wedding cookies and flaming-hot Mexican coffee served in molded chocolate cups and saucers or flowerpots. (See *Supplier Resource Directory* for sources.)

Anniversary Gift Suggestions

Choose one of these very special ninth anniversary gifts:
- Piece of pottery
- Potted plant
- Willow basket filled with fruit or flowers
- Copy of the movie *Ghost*
- Pottery class for two
- Clay cooking pans or bowls

- Classic, leather-bound book or leather photo album (Leather is listed on many anniversary lists as the modern choice. Refer to "The Third Anniversary: Leather" chapter for more leather gift ideas.)

A Special Moment for the Anniversary Couple

Botanical Garden Tête-à-Tête

Orchestrate a romantic tête-à-tête in a commercial greenhouse, lush conservatory, or public botanical garden among flowering potted plants and soft classical music. Set out a candlelight dinner-for-two table or romantic picnic-basket lunch. Arrange for a violin serenade or dance to a string quartet.

The Tenth Anniversary
—Tin—

*Toast: Salute Robert and Tamala with "tin"
anniversary congratulations!*

Congratulations to the ten-year anniversary couple! Celebrate this noteworthy achievement with delightful tin-can charm or with a glittering Tinsel Town (Hollywood) party. You could also celebrate the tenth anniversary in contemporary fashion with the modern tenth anniversary designation—diamonds! Although diamonds are traditionally the sixtieth-and-beyond wedding anniversary designation, a couple may not want to wait that long. Besides, why not celebrate with diamonds twice?

Tin-Can Charm

This is a charming and nostalgic "tin" anniversary party to share with close friends and family members.

Invitation Ideas

Invite guests to the party with tin-can charm.

- Wrap an invitation label around the outside of a tin (aluminum) can.
- Tie a set of metal measuring spoons to the corner of a printed invitation with a silver curly ribbon.

- Attach a small card containing party details to a metal cookie cutter with a pretty ribbon.
- Place a party invitation inside an antique advertising-tin container.
- Glue the invitation to the inside of a pie tin.
- Write details on a post card or note card picturing the Tin Man from *The Wizard of Oz.*
- Decorate the outside of an invitation with aluminum tooling foil. Using a hobby-hole-punch tool, punch a heart design or the word "Tin" into the foil before gluing it to the card.

Special Instructions for Guests

In honor of Andrea and John's "Tin" Anniversary, please bring a box of canned goods to be donated to the local homeless shelter.

Decorating Touches

Cover the party area in tin.

- Cover the table with an aluminum foil tablecloth.
- Cover the wall behind the table (or party room walls) with aluminum foil or silver shimmering decorative curtains (sold with party supplies).
- Stack aluminum cans (labels removed) in several groupings at different heights on the table. Drape twinkle lights over and around the cans and add small votive glass candles to make the arrangement sparkle.
- Hang a tin man made with empty tin cans at the front door and add a "Happy Tin Anniversary" banner.
- Line the driveway and a path to the front door with tin can luminarias (tin cans filled with sand and candles). These are also great for outlining patio and deck areas.
- Cover patio tables with a variety of colored gingham-checked cloths. Add coordinating solid napkins with metal cookie cutters as napkin rings.
- Make aluminum coffeepot lanterns for centerpieces. Purchase second-hand vintage coffeepots and drill ¼- or ½-inch holes in the side of the pot using a metal drill bit. Using acrylic enamel, paint the handles and lid of each coffeepot to match the color of one of the gingham-checked tablecloths.

- Fill a glass cookie jar with tin cookie cutters or foil-wrapped candy. Tie with a fancy bow and use as a table centerpiece.
- Use pie tins (metal or aluminum foil) as dinner plates.
- Purchase tin cups from a camping supplier, army surplus store, or Civil War vendor listed in the *Supplier Resource Directory.*
- Use one or a collection of the following antique tin treasures as a table or buffet centerpiece: advertising tins, tin chocolate molds, tin soldiers, tin toys, and tin banks.
- Use children's antique sand pails painted with colorful beach designs as centerpieces or fill them with napkins, utensils, or dinner rolls. Line the pails with a colorful napkin before adding the food.
- Decorate the area or tables with tin-can planters and metal watering cans, colanders, funnels, or flour sifters.
- Fill the air with fragrant spices by heating tin pans of potpourri.
- Fill a new aluminum garbage can with ice and party brews.

Theme-Inspired Activities and Entertainment

Now, for some tin-can thrills:
- Toss Frisbee pie tins or aluminum foil pie plates back and forth.
- Play toss games using empty tin cans.
- Go on a tin-can recycling hunt or a hunt for more canned goods to donate to a local charity.
- Gather guests into the kitchen for one of these tin-cooking fun ideas: Make and bake pies, roll out cookie dough and cut out fun shapes with tin cookie cutters, or make chocolates with tin candy molds.
- Hire a "Tin Pan Alley" band to play current dance music.
- Hold a pie-eating contest.
- Show a tin man video such as *The Wizard of Oz* or *Tin Man.*

Menu Ideas

Prepare a tin-wrapped menu of delights.

- Wrap a Virginia ham in aluminum foil before baking. Serve sliced ham sandwiches with honey mustard on an assortment of sandwich breads: onion rolls, rye, pumpernickel, white, wheat, bagels, and croissants.
- Serve baked potatoes that have been coated with butter, wrapped with bacon, and then encased in aluminum foil for baking.
- Cook baked beans in the can on the kitchen or campfire stove top.
- Roast corn on the cob wrapped in aluminum foil over coals on an outside grill.
- Bake the anniversary cake in a pie tin. Crown it with a heart or "T-I-N" design cake topper made from aluminum tooling foil.

Party Favors with Flair

Plan to give each guest a "tinny" anniversary memento.

- Metal cookie-cutter candy favor (Cut out a cardboard shape using the metal cookie cutter. Glue it to the back of the cookie cutter. Then, placing the cookie cutter flat against a table, fill it with candy. Finally, slip it into a cellophane bag and tie it with a pretty ribbon.)
- Homemade pie
- Aluminum-foil-wrapped photo frame
- Foil-wrapped molded chocolates, perhaps in a tin-soldier design
- Tin whistle
- Five-and-dime store items

Tinsel Town Party

Invite guests to become celebrity stars for a night at a Tinsel Town Party, an evening of Hollywood-premiere-style glamour, by sending the invitation inside a large, metal movie-film canister or VCR tape case (see *Supplier Resource Directory*). Make your invitations by covering an empty VCR tape case with a specially designed "Tinsel Town Party" advertisement jacket. Place a packet of microwave popcorn inside the container.

Pick up guests from their homes or from one meeting location and transport them to the party in stretch limousines. Rent a roving spotlight to mark the Tinsel Town party location. Roll out the red carpet (literally) with all its glamorous treatment for star-studded guests. Hand guests Hollywood shades (sunglasses favors) when they arrive. They'll need these to protect themselves from Tinsel Town shine and to look "Hollywood cool." As celebrity guests arrive, they will have their fifteen minutes of fame as "reporters" shoot their photos. Also, plan for a "camera crew" to be on hand to record candid video memories and best wishes to the anniversary couple. You could even project the arriving "celebrity stars" on a large screen TV or movie screen. Play these recordings back during a late-night screening.

Once inside, serve guests celebrity cocktails with white-gloved, silver-tray service. Offer "Charlie Chaplin" champagne, "Make-My-Day" margaritas, Madonna's "Like-a-Virgin" cocktails, and "Bette Davis Eyes" Daiquiris. Present the anniversary couple with an autograph book to take around the room and collect "celebrity" (party guests') signatures, a perfect mingling activity.

Decorate the party area with sparkling Tinsel Town splendor. Cover tables with floor-length silver lamé cloths. Use black chair covers wrapped with silver lamé chair sashes. Attach sparkling silver stars on the chair backs, printed with each guest's name. For more Hollywood fun, use the names of famous Hollywood stars and let guests choose their seats.

Place a silver-and-glitter-framed photo of the anniversary couple in the center of the table. Surround it with decorative silver tinsel and glowing votive candlelight. Add a movie clapboard with "Ted and Nancy's Tinsel Town Anniversary" as the current movie scene. Place disposable cameras at each place setting for guests to capture glimpses of celebrity look-a-likes mingling at the party. Encircle the room with silver metallic Christmas trees and hang silver-and-glitter-framed movie posters on the walls. For an added "Hollywood star" touch, hang stars on "dressing" room doors—the men's and women's restrooms.

Show the party movie trailer—the anniversary best wishes and candid takes of arriving guests—on a big screen. Then open "the envelope" and present the anniversary couple with an "And the winner is . . ." Hollywood anniversary award. More Hollywood ceremony follows. Have the anniversary couple place their handprints and autographs on the Mann's Chinese Theater walk of fame. Display the couple's handprints and signatures on a giant anniversary cake.

Anniversary Gift Suggestions

Choose a special tin-inspired gift for this tenth anniversary:

- Set of vintage, vividly colored aluminum beverage tumblers
- Tin photo frame
- Antique advertising nostalgia tins
- Antique tin soldiers, tin toys, or tin banks
- Tin candlesticks
- Decorative tin filled with "tin-covered" Hershey's Kisses
- Borrow from the modern tenth anniversary gift designation—diamonds —for special gifts for the anniversary couple. Wrap a diamond tennis bracelet around a tin can or place a man's diamond ring inside an empty tin can.

A Special Moment for the Anniversary Couple

Tin Lizzie Fun

Kidnap your spouse in a rented "Tin Lizzie" Ford for a romantic "tin can" picnic complete with canned oysters and chilled, tin-can-served champagne. Or, step out for a Tinsel Town night—a Hollywood movie, a five-star-restaurant meal, and some Fred Astaire and Ginger Rogers dancing. Contact a local classic-car club about arranging a chauffeured rental.

The Eleventh Anniversary
—Steel—

Toast: Here's to "steel" lovin' you after all these years!

After eleven years of marriage, the union has become strong as steel. Steel, a symbol of strength, also plays an instrumental role in the romantic sounds of the steel guitar and the free-and-easy beat of the steel drum. Celebrate this steel anniversary with the mystique of the Hawaiian guitar, the down-home twang of the country and western steel guitar, or the tropical island sound of the Jamaican steel drum.

Steel Lovin' You Honky-Tonk

Love sometimes mimics a country and western song—the jingle-jangle of love-struck bliss, or the "tears-in-your-beers" twang of the lonely blues. The anniversary couple manages to "steel" keep on lovin', and they deserve to enjoy some down-home party fun to celebrate a marriage that's "strong as steel."

Invitation Ideas

Invite country and western music lovers (and haters) to this honky-tonk anniversary celebration with hillbilly music flair:

- Send invitation details attached to a corncob pipe.
- Write and record a song over a recorded, popular country and western tune. (See the *Supplier Resource Directory* for an inexpensive, easy to obtain, music recording license.) Include invitation details in the lyrics as well as a written copy in the cassette tape cover.
- Write invitation details on the back of a post card showing the Grand Ole Opry stage.
- Attach invitation details to a bag of chewing tobacco or chewing tobacco bubble gum.
- Send a decorative bag or box filled with "bluegrass" (blue paper or Mylar gift-wrapping shreds). Label it with this invitation message: "You're invited to an anniversary celebration filled with some down-home country and western *bluegrass* fun."
- Place an engraved invitation inside a Mason jar marked with a "White Lightnin'" label.
- Attach a misspelled "Y'all Nvited" sign to a Lil' Abner comic book.
- Send a box of steel-wool cleaning pads with a note reading, *"Steel* Loving You Eleventh Anniversary Party."
- Paint a small toy guitar (or guitar-shaped ornament) steel colored and attach it to a "Steel *Gee*-tar Fun" invitation message.

Special Instructions for Guests

Wear your tackiest and tawdriest country and western entertainer costumes—Texas-tall hair, fringe, cowboy boots, flashy rhinestones, and so on. There will be an award ceremony for the "Tackiest Country and Western Star" costume.

Decorating Touches

Decorate with hillbilly honky-tonk flair. Hold the party in a local honky-tonk (country and western bar) or create a roadhouse atmosphere.

- Set uncovered tables with unique hill-country vases filled with wild-flowers. Use beer bottles, Mountain Dew soda pop bottles, or Mason jars.
- Attach dangling price tags to straw hats for Minnie Pearl hat centerpieces.

- Line the back of the bar with crock jugs labeled "moonshine" and "white lightnin'."
- Set an antique ringer-washer out on the porch with a sign reading, "*Steel* Lovin' You Honky-Tonk." Next to this, situate several hillbilly-costumed actors (or friends and family members) in rocking chairs, with some holding framed photos of the anniversary couple.
- Decorate the walls with country-and-western-singer posters and album covers. Add neon beer advertisement signs. Also, include rhinestone-covered western boots and shirts on the wall.
- Decorate the outside of the men's and women's restrooms to resemble the door of an outhouse, complete with a moon cut-out window.
- Serve moonshine drinks in wide-mouthed Mason jars.

Theme-Inspired Activities and Entertainment

Country and western singer Jim Reeves once said, "The shortest distance between two hearts is a song." Create a Grand Ole Opry lineup of country music, filled with country and western love songs and steel guitar tunes.

- Hold a karaoke contest featuring sad country and western songs.
- Hire a country and western dance band.
- Stage a country and western music awards presentation for the "Tackiest Dressed Star" as described in the *Special Instructions for Guests* section.
- Pitch horseshoes out back.
- Hold pie-eating and "sooey" (pig-calling) contests.
- Stage a blindfolded beer-tasting identification contest.
- Hold a shotgun anniversary wedding photo opportunity. Have friends and family stand in front of the preacher with the bride and groom (anniversary couple) for photo opportunities. Don't forget to have a father figure holding a shotgun to the groom's back.
- Hold a tobacco spittin' contest, spitting bubble gum wads into a steel spittoon (coffee can).
- Take guests on a moonlight hayride.

Menu Ideas

Put out a honky-tonk buffet spread displayed in cut-out guitars and drums. Surround these singular pieces with additional musical instruments and autographed celebrity photos. Feature a Grand Ole Opry, all-star lineup menu including the following:

- Loretta Lynn strawberry and bananas Jell-O heart mold
- Grandpa Jones roast barbecued pork
- Tammy Wynette "Stand By Your Man" mashed potatoes
- Green peas and Minnie Pearl onions
- Slim Pickens barbecued baked beans
- Hank Williams "Your Cheatin' Heart" heart-shaped biscuits and cornbread
- Patsy Cline "Sweet Dreams" make-your-own sundae bar
- Guitar-shaped wedding anniversary cake

Party Favors with Flair

"Steel" guests' hearts with just the right party favor memento.

- Shotgun anniversary wedding instant photos and country and western music karaoke videos described in the *Theme-Inspired Activities and Entertainment* section above
- Corncob pipe
- Brown wrapper or country-and-western-designed gift bag filled with blue-colored gift-wrap "grass" (paper or Mylar shreds) and a bluegrass tape or CD labeled "Bluegrass Party Favor"
- Ribbon-wrapped Grand Ole Opry note cards
- Bag of bubble gum chewing tobacco
- Ribbon-tied bottle of Mountain Dew
- Lil' Abner comic book tied with a misspelled "Y'all Come Bak" note.
- Bandanna tied with a simple ribbon and filled with "steelies."

Jamaican Steel Drum Jammin'

Yaw Mon! It's Jamaican Jammin' time! Cast a spell of carefree fun and mystical love-voodoo with the jammin' beat of the steel drum. Invite guests to this spellbinding affair with "charming" invitations. Send a voodoo doll stuck with steel "love" pins (straight pins glued to "love-inscribed" paper hearts).

Celebrate this anniversary party at the beach or by a pool. Sip Jamaican rum and colas under a thatched roof beach bar, complete with a macaw mascot. Fill galvanized steel garbage cans (new and sanitized, of course) with ice, sodas, and Jamaican ginger beer. Sit at cocktail tables made by covering steel oil drums with varnished table-tops. Make centerpieces using wooden bowls of fruit or tall, colored love-potion bottles. Enjoy tropically inspired fare such as coconut shrimp, seafood salad served in avocado halves, Caribbean chicken marinated in spicy Jamaican jammin' sauce, bananas flambé, and a coconut-covered pineapple upside-down anniversary cake. Place the steel drum music band on a floating stage over the pool. Dance to reggae music and include a little limbo-dancing fun.

Anniversary on the Steel Track Express

All aboard the Steel Track Express for an anniversary adventure to various mysterious destinations. This party honors the opulence of the Orient Express. Invite guests with the following message: "The Steel Track Express Anniversary Train" will depart (date) from (host's name) Grand Central Station at (address) promptly at (time)." Send this message with one of these unusual train party favors: a small toy train, a train whistle, or a conductor's hat. As a unique expression, fold and place invitation details inside a luggage tag, paste details inside an Orient Express travel brochure, or design an invitation that resembles a passport. Keep the train stop destination a mystery. If you like, ask guests to come dressed as these famous detectives to fit the mysterious Orient Express ambiance: Charlie Chan, Sherlock Holmes, Hercule Poirot, or Miss Marple.

The original Orient Express started in Paris and traveled to Venice and Istanbul, the "gateway to the Orient." Your anniversary train can travel to any destination of your choice—real or imagined—and any time period. You'll want to decorate, serve refreshments, and provide activities corresponding to each destination stop. We've chosen one itinerary of romantic secret destinations: China, England, and Ancient Egypt.

Gather guests at "Grand Central Station" (the host's or anniversary couple's home). Get on track for the trip by playing "Chattanooga Choo Choo" and other fun forties train tunes. From a "ticket booth" or "souvenir window," distribute disposable cameras for collecting travel shots along the way. In truly over-the-top Orient Express opulence, offer waiting passengers Kir Royals served in cut-crystal champagne flutes.

Collect previously requested "passports." (These current photos of each guest will be used later in a passport portfolio presentation to the anniversary couple.) Board passengers onto the Steel Track Express Anniversary Train—chauffeured carpools, vans, or luxurious limousines. It's also fun to "all aboard" the entire party onto specially chartered buses or even a real train. Now, it's off to our first exotic destination!

Stop #1—China

Step off the "train" and visit a local Chinese restaurant or your most honorable China room. Decorate the walls with Chinese bamboo paintings and Chinese travel posters. Crisscross a string of Chinese lanterns across the ceiling. Cover guests' tables with red chinoiserie-patterned silk cloths. Use a floral-filled Chinese takeout carton or an exotic Chinese vase and fan combination as the centerpiece. A goldfish bowl filled with scotch broom and swimming goldfish also makes an exotic statement. Scatter fortune cookies around the base of either centerpiece. Hire a mandolinist or play recorded, mood-setting Chinese music. Serve Chinese hors d'oeuvres on this first train stop: mini egg rolls with sweet-and-sour or hot mustard sauce, crab and cream cheese fried wontons, and pot stickers (a fried dough and pork combination). Also, serve honorable guests hot Chinese tea. Invite them to take a pair of decorative chopsticks as a memento of this alluring Chinatown stop. Then reboard passengers onto the Orient Express for the next mystery destination.

Stop #2 — England

Now, it's off to an English pub for a jolly good main-course time. Create an English pub atmosphere in a local corner bar or restaurant. Hang dart boards and London-sites posters on the walls. Cover tables with British flags as tablecloths. Set out an authentic-looking red British phone booth for impromptu photo opportunities. Direct passengers to this English pub with English bobby characters. Once in the pub, entertain guests with royal hospitality. Have a Queen Elizabeth II look-alike receive guests at the entrance. Be sure to inform guests ahead of time of the proper royal protocol. Play Beatles tunes and surprise guests with a look-alike visit from the Fab Four. Provide a small dance floor for "twisting and shouting." For this main-course stop, serve fish and chips (French fries) with malt vinegar and salt. Like a true Londoner, wrap the fish and chips in newspaper. Offer yards of ale and china teacups filled with Earl Grey tea. Give passengers miniature British flags to wave good-bye to this royal stop. It's time now to board the train for the final mystery destination.

Stop #3 — Ancient Egypt

Passengers disembark back in time at our final destination along the Nile River in Ancient Egypt. Invite passengers inside an ancient Egyptian nightclub decorated with posters of camels, the Sphinx, and the Pyramids. Prop up a mummy in its sarcophagus against the wall. Add pillars set with large Egyptian cat figures surrounded by large ferns around the room. Cover cocktail tables with white butcher paper and crayons, instructing passengers to draw Egyptian hieroglyphics. Set an "Elixir" bottle in the center of each table. Make the youth potion with a chilled bottle of champagne, hanging an "Elixir" label around its neck. Place rustic stoneware goblets around the bottle for a champagne toast to the anniversary couple. Entertain guests with ancient Egyptian flair. Play Egyptian music in the background. Conduct a cake-cutting ceremony, having an Egyptian-clad wait staff serve pieces of King-Tut-decorated anniversary cake to each guest. Propose a special toast to the anniversary couple with the "Elixir" champagne. Next, present the anniversary couple with the passport portfolio—a collection of guest "passport" photos. Send guests home with their eleventh anniversary vacation photo cameras and a gift certificate for developing the film. Pyramid-shaped perfume bottles would also make a nice gift.

Anniversary Gift Suggestions

Here are some "Steel lovin' you" gift suggestions along with some "Jamaican steel drum jammin'" and "steel blue Hawaiian splendor" ideas:

- Galvanized steel bucket filled with country and western love song cassettes or CDs
- Pair of country and western music concert tickets
- Case of the couple's favorite beer marked "White Lightnin'"
- Brand-new, shiny metal garbage can filled with Jamaican-bright colored beach towels, a bottle of Jamaican rum, and a steel drum music CD or cassette.
- Bird of paradise flower plant
- Set of steel blue bed sheets
- Set of stainless steel flatware
- Steel beach pail filled with seashells and a bottle of champagne
- Steel blue gift bag or box filled with macadamia nut cookies and a Hawaiian steel guitar cassette or CD
- Matching set of steel-blue-faced watches, adjoining heart-half key chains, or other fashion jewelry sets (Fashion jewelry is often listed as the modern gift suggestion for the eleventh anniversary.)

A Special Moment for the Anniversary Couple

Steel Wheels Escape

"Steel" your spouse away for an anniversary celebration in a steel-wheeled stretch-limousine. Pack the limousine with metallic silver, helium-filled Mylar balloons. Include a bottle of champagne over ice in a steel bucket and play "Steel lovin' you" music including "your" song. Then roll away for "steel" more anniversary romance.

The Twelfth Anniversary
—Silk—

Toast: May the road ahead of you be smooth as silk!

The pleasures of a twelve-year marriage are as luxurious as silk. This anniversary party calls for silken fantasies. Imagine the dance of the seven veils in an Arabian gambling den or the Far East mystique of a Silken Fantasies party. Still more fun lies behind the lurking suspense of a *Silk Stalkings* murder mystery party.

Linen-themed parties are also commonly associated with the twelfth anniversary. Linen, a popular Irish commodity, often represents Ireland's merriment. For your anniversary shenanigans, cover party tables in fine Irish linen and add some of the Irish accents showcased in the fifty-fifth anniversary chapter.

Silken Fantasies

Create a silken anniversary fantasy shrouded in Far East mystique. Surround guests with the beauty of Japanese silk fans, the delicate scent of jasmine, and the drifting sound of oriental strings.

Invitation Ideas

Invite guests with one of these silky oriental touches:

- Write details on—or include a note with—a silk Japanese fan.
- Attach the invitation to a small silk pillow wrapped with silk ribbons.
- Write invitation details on the outside of a Japanese accordion-like paper lantern. Use the Japanese writing style and print vertically.
- Include the words "Most Honorable Guest" on the invitation.
- Attach a piece of pretty Japanese-design silk fabric to the invitation.
- Lace a silk ribbon through the edges of the invitation.

Special Instructions for Guests

Invite guests to wear something silk to the party. The item doesn't have to be visible. Ask guests to bring their fantasy to the party. Enclose a blank fan-shaped card that guests will use to record a fantasy dream or wish.

Decorating Touches

Cover the room with the silken Far East mystique of a Japanese tearoom.

- To create the *fantasy* atmosphere, place silk Japanese fans everywhere. Place fans on guest tables, walls, furniture, window cornices, buffets—just about every available square inch of the party area.
- Outside, hang long, flowing silk ribbons from tree branches.
- Surround the party area with an oriental silk-screen enclosure.
- Cover low guest tables with silk cloths and arrange silk pillows around them for guest seating.
- Set the table with Japanese china table settings including teapots and teacups.
- Lay a set of chopsticks near a silk napkin folded into a fan shape.
- Place a Japanese fan across each guest's plate.
- Add Buddha statues and running fountains filled with swimming goldfish to the party area.
- Attach Japan travel posters, paper dragons, and silk kimonos to the wall.

- Hang paper lanterns and silk Japanese-design parasols from the ceiling.
- Pair silk fan centerpieces with Japanese dolls, silk high-heeled shoes filled with apple-blossom branches, or silk Japanese lanterns. Goldfish swimming in a low, black-lacquered square bowl also make a distinctive centerpiece.

Theme-Inspired Activities and Entertainment

Treat guests to "pleasures of the Far East" from the moment they walk into the anniversary party.

- Announce the arrival of each guest with the strike of a ceremonial gong.
- Greet guests with a receiving line of geisha-costumed characters. The greeters will present each guest with a silk kimono to wear at the party. Rent a kimono for each guest from costume shops or honor each guest with a kimono gift.
- Gently remind guests to observe the ancient Japanese custom of removing shoes before entering the hospitality area.
- Play the dramatic music from *Madame Butterfly*.
- Pour half a bag of rice into a silk cloth square and securely tie the ends together. Pass this silk bundle around the party and, without opening it, have guests feel and guess the number of rice pieces inside.
- Observe this unusual sake custom in which overpouring is a sign of generosity. Pour hot sake into a small black-lacquered box, overfilling it and spilling some sake onto the saucer. Instruct each guest to sip the sake from the box without lifting it. Once the box is partially emptied, pour the spilled sake from the saucer back into the box and lift the box to drink.
- Read aloud the fantasy cards brought by guests and described in the *Special Instructions for Guests* section.

Menu Ideas

In Japan, exquisitely arranged boxes of sushi are bought to take home, just as Westerners buy and take home boxes of chocolates. Bring in a sushi chef to artfully prepare and serve sushi from a sushi bar as hors d'oeuvres. In addition, serve a dinner of hospitable Japanese flavor.

- Sashimi, raw fish sliced paper-thin and garnished with shredded carrot and cabbage salad
- Variety of seafood and vegetable tempura
- Teriyaki chicken and beef
- Yakitori (bite-sized grilled chicken pieces on skewers)
- Onigariyaki (large marinated and grilled prawn halves)
- Japanese rice and vegetables
- Green tea
- Plum wine
- Hot sake served as described in the *Theme-Inspired Activities and Entertainment* section
- Vanilla ice cream served with a bean curd topping

Party Favors with Flair

Wrap party favors in silk cloth with the art of furoshiki. Fold a silk scarf around the gift object and then tie the scarf ends together in decorative knots. This decorative wrap is reminiscent of the ancient tradition of tsutsumi in which gifts were wrapped in a particular color, knot, or fold to symbolize the occasion. Wrap one of these selections in silken fantasy:

- Spun sugar fantasy candy (It looks like wavy curves of silk ribbon.)
- Bottle of sake or plum wine
- Decorative tin of green tea
- Japanese doll
- Single silky rose
- Silk Japanese fan
- Silk kimono distributed upon arrival

Arabian Gambling Den

Invite guests to an anniversary celebration full of Arabian Nights romance. Create an Arabian gambling den atmosphere with a night of casino games and middle eastern mystique. Enclose two or three poker chips with a party invitation that includes these special instructions: "The secret password is *camel*." Guard the outside of the gambling den with threatening characters dressed in business suits, desert headdress, dark sunglasses, and machine guns (toy, of course).

Guests will enter a gambling den draped with rich colors. Surround the guests with casino game excitement and tables covered in silk. Add intimate conversation areas decorated with Persian rugs and large silk floor pillows. Place brass bowls of fruit on the floor and offer instant photo opportunities.

On a low stage, tucked in a den corner, charm guests with the dance of the seven veils and belly dance entertainment. Indulge guests with midnight supper hors d'oeuvres including caviar toast triangles, sugar-glazed grapes, and sparkling champagne. Then uncover a delectable "Seven Deadly Sins" dessert buffet.

Silk Stalkings

Murder stalks this night of mystery and intrigue. Beware, the suspense may kill you. Invite guests to an evening of intrigue by sending a silk stocking (lady's nylon hose) with the invitation. Hang silk stockings from tree branches, on the front door, and around the room. Greet guests with a "the butler did it" character and invite them in for "whodunit?" "whydunit?" and "howdunit?" fun.

Set up fondue stations on various tables around the room. Cover each table with a different colored silk tablecloth trimmed with dangling silk stockings. Guests rotate from table to table enjoying each station's special-recipe fondue pot. They dip bread pieces into a cheese fondue at one station. They cook vegetable or meat pieces in oil at two other stations that also provide a variety of dipping sauces. Then they dip fruit pieces, marshmallows, and pound-cake pieces at a chocolate fondue station.

Also, print the "fondue tradition" on a card attached to a silk stocking and thrown across each fondue table. Tradition requires that if a lady drops a piece of food from her fondue fork, she must kiss the gentleman to her left. If a gentleman drops a piece, he must buy a bottle of wine. As guests get thirsty, perhaps a "gentleman" will drop a piece from his fondue fork. Place a "collection" jar next to a line of wine bottles placed on a sideboard table. A gift certificate for the anniversary couple will be purchased with the money collected there.

The party plan is "elementary, my dear." Assign character dossiers and invite guests to come in character using a murder mystery game package. You can also hire a murder mystery entertainment company to stage a "murder" in front of the guests. Or, stalk the murder suspects and examine their alibis while putting together the murder mystery puzzle. Award the winner a Slinky toy for his or her "slinky" sleuthing. Wrap the prize in a silk stocking, of course!

Anniversary Gift Suggestions

- Japanese silk wall hanging
- Set of silk sheets
- Decorative silk pillows
- Matching silk kimonos
- Large Japanese-fan wall decoration
- Cassette or CD of Japanese music
- Tickets to *Madame Butterfly*
- His-and-her monogrammed silk shirts
- His-and-her silk pajama sets
- Pair of silk umbrellas
- Lamp with a silk lampshade
- Silk lingerie, as a gift between the couple
- Silk hankie or scarf, as a gift from husband to wife
- Silk tie, as a gift from wife to husband
- Mother-of-pearl inlaid photo frame or memory box (Pearl is the modern gift designation for the twelfth anniversary. For more "pearly" gift ideas, see "The Thirtieth Anniversary: Pearl" chapter.)

A Special Moment for the Anniversary Couple

Silk Pillow Talk

Drop the kids off at Grandma's and let the answering machine pick up the telephone. It's time for some romantic pillow talk. Cover the bedroom in nothing more than soft candlelight, romantic music, and luxurious silk sheets. Prop up silk pillows to watch Doris Day and Rock Hudson in the film *Pillow Talk*. Or, choose another romantic classic—maybe some pillow talk of your own!

The Thirteenth Anniversary
—Lace—

*Toast: May you treasure your love
like beautiful, delicate lace.*

The number thirteen is seldom seen as lucky—except for this occasion. People are often superstitious about the number thirteen, which affects customs in many ways. The French never issue thirteen as a house address. National and international airlines omit numbering a thirteenth row. And it's rare to find a thirteenth floor in a high-rise building in the United States. However, a thirteen-year marriage should be appreciated and cherished. Treasured lace—with its fine beauty—perfectly symbolizes a warm and loving thirteen-year relationship. Trim this anniversary in lace sentiment with one of the following parties.

Arsenic and Old Lace Tea

The sweet charm of this anniversary tea is laced with the murder mystery from Frank Capra's movie *Arsenic and Old Lace*. The outlandish tale portrays two sweet and gentle, yet lethal, little old ladies who poison lonely old men as an apparent act of charity. The diabolical deeds are done while entertaining with proper etiquette, of course.

Invitation Ideas

You'll want to send a "proper" afternoon tea invitation. Here are a few lacy suggestions:

- Pretty lacy handkerchief tucked inside an engraved invitation
- Delicate square paper doily with its corners folded in and laced together with a silk ribbon (Write invitation details directly on the inside of the doily.)
- Small corked bottle decorated with lace and a tag reading, "Arsenic and Old Lace"
- Lace-trimmed invitation placed inside a pretty teacup
- Tea bag with an "Arsenic and Old Lace" tag

Special Instructions for Guests

Devise and bring a plan for the perfect murder. A card is enclosed for your convenience. (Hint: Include the perfect weapon, alibi, and cunning procedure.)

Decorating Touches

An afternoon tea, even a murderous one, should be set with care and dignity.

- Lace decorates every room. Hang lace curtains on the windows. Place crocheted lace doilies on coffee and end tables. Throw a Chantilly lace tablecloth over the living room davenport. Accent overstuffed chairs with lacy pillows. Hang lace-edged guest towels in the bathroom.
- Cover an antique side buffet with a fine lace or antique crocheted table runner.
- Lace and more lace accentuate a romantic dining room table set with a buffet tea service. Set a silver tea service at one end of the table and a silver coffee service at the other end. As is customary, place a chair near each service and ask a close friend or family member to

serve. Take away all the other chairs. Fill the center of the table with plates of teacakes and fancies.

- Place a lace-trimmed tea napkin through the handle of each china teacup.

- Set individual tea tables with tête-à-tête intimacy. Cover small tables with fine lace or lace-trimmed cloths. A ruffled eyelet lace pillow sham makes a delightful tea tablecloth. For lovely centerpieces, fill china teapots with fresh flowers, perhaps fragrant lilacs or lilies of the valley. Another centerpiece idea is filling a vintage handbag with a low vase of fresh or silk flowers. Conceal the vase with florist's moss. Drape a pretty pair of vintage lady's gloves and a strand of pearls over the open handbag edge. Next to the centerpieces at each table, place a different murder weapon such as a candlestick, a revolver (toy, of course), a knife, a piece of rope, and so on. Lay lace flower blooms at each place setting, rolling lace cloths or hankies into flower shapes and attaching them to floral stems.

- Make a lace cake centerpiece. Stack two large rolls of white- or cream-colored crepe paper and cover them with lace. Top the lace confection with silk roses and trim the bottom edge with silk ribbon. Display it on a pretty cake plate.

- Remember the elderly sisters' temporary "resting" place for their murder victims? It was the window box seat. Place your window box seat near one of the windows and drape it with a lace cloth. Presents for the couple—or sitting "bodies"—can gather here.

Theme-Inspired Activities and Entertainment

Entertain anniversary guests with charming afternoon tea conversation and a little murder mayhem.

- Have two elderly sister characters dressed in lacy old-fashioned apparel invite guests into the tea parlor. They can politely offer guests a glass of "laced" wine, pointing to a lace-draped table displaying a crystal decanter of wine and lace-appliquéd wineglasses. Hang a small lace-trimmed card around the decanter reading, "Laced."

- Or, hire two little old lady character entertainers (using costumed men is hilarious) who serve guests tea while "hiding" a dead body (prop) under the table.

- The plot thickens with more movie-inspired, walk-around entertainers: a bizarre "Teddy Roosevelt" brother character, a long lost diabolical brother, and a demented plastic surgeon.

- The quirky sisters in the movie always buried the poor lonely old men with a "proper" ceremony. You, too, might want to conduct a proper ceremony. Toast the couple with the laced wine (described above) and stage a eulogy. Read aloud the murder plot cards brought by guests (as described in the *Special Instructions for Guests* section). After reading and discussing each one, you may want to bury the "evidence" in the cellar or backyard. To be proper, have a lace-bow-trimmed shovel on hand for the occasion.

- Play mood-setting classical "tea" music, such as Handel's *Hornpipe*, in the background.

- Plan a unique seating-assignment activity using the question "What weapon did Professor Plum use to kill Miss Scarlet in the observatory?" Tie small place cards around each napkin using a pretty satin ribbon. Inscribe each card with the name of a Clue-game murder weapon (candlestick, knife, revolver, and so on). You can also attach an actual Clue-game playing card or charm. Ask guests to match their cards to corresponding weapons placed on various tables or at individual place settings.

- Use the same Clue-game charm for a table favor prize drawing. Place Clue-game charms depicting murder weapons inside lace English party favor crackers. Draw Clue-game cards and award door prizes to those holding matching charms. Make party crackers by rolling a bathroom tissue tube in white crepe or tissue gift-wrap. Cut the paper three inches longer at each end of the tube. Tie the ends with delicate satin ribbons and wrap the center with antique white or ecru lace.

- Play parlor games for the guests' amusement. Charades would be fun—guessing famous murder mystery movies and book titles. Pictionary or an Old Maid card game might also be entertaining.

- Offer quiet corners for old-fashioned parlor handholding.

- For those who "make it" through the afternoon tea and want to hang around for more murder mayhem, play the movie *Arsenic and Old Lace,* starring Cary Grant.

Menu Ideas

Place dainty tea sandwiches and other teatime treats on paper-lace-doily-trimmed silver trays, antique glass plates, and tiered china serving pieces.

- Tea sandwiches: Victorian cucumber, smoked salmon pinwheels, and tiny chicken salad croissants
- Currant scones served with thick and creamy Devonshire clotted cream and homemade strawberry jam
- Coconut macaroons, ladyfingers, and tiny cream puffs
- Lacy looking cakes and cookies (Top cakes with powdered-sugar-sprinkled lace designs, made by sprinkling powdered sugar over paper lace doilies. Rosette cookies sprinkled with powdered sugar are another lacy looking option.)
- Chocolate-dipped strawberries
- Pastel-colored petits fours displayed on the blades of large, murder-inspired chopping knives
- Steaming hot Earl Grey tea and rose-petal tea
- Punch served from an elegant punch bowl labeled "Arsenic-Laced"

Party Favors with Flair

Even without one of these delightful party mementos, guests won't forget this murder-laced afternoon tea experience.

- Lace hankie bundled with decorated sugar cubes or candies and tied with a delicate satin ribbon (Paint sugar cubes with tiny frosting flowers and hearts.)
- China teacup with a lace hankie slipped through the handle (If you like, plant a flower in—or add a silk floral arrangement to—the cup.)
- Candy-filled corked bottle trimmed with lace and a small placard reading, "Arsenic and Old Lace"
- Lace-wrapped bundle of tea bags trimmed with a satin ribbon and an "Arsenic and Old Lace" tag
- Single handmade rose, its bloom made with a lace hankie
- Molded chocolate teacup presented in clear cellophane wrap and tied with a lace bow (See *Supplier Resource Directory*.)

Denim and Lace Barn Dance

It's well known that opposites attract. Here's a contrasting pair that makes a really exciting combination—denim and lace. Prim and proper lace, with its pretty and feminine look, contrasts with the casual, down-home look of denim. This exceptional duo provides a delightful theme for any anniversary party from barbecues to formal balls. Stage this "lucky thirteen" anniversary celebration with a delightful old-fashioned barn dance.

Invite guests to wear denim and lace. Attach an invitation to denim-and-lace cloth pieces tied together into a love knot. Another unique invitation idea is a Levi pocket holding a lace-trimmed invitation.

Hold this old-homestead dance in a barn, rustic event hall, or even a backyard. Greet guests with some old-fashioned fiddle playing. Throw hay on the floor and bring in hay bales for seating. Line the walls with a mural of farm creatures such as cows, chickens, and pigs. Add hay forks and tractor wheel accents. Drive in a tractor for fun photo opportunities. Hang Levi's and jean jackets, with delicate lace hankies sticking out of the pockets, on the walls as decorations.

Drape delicate lace cloth from the ceiling or rafters and over windows. Wrap lace around pillars. Cover rustic-looking wood picnic tables with denim and lace charm. Lay fine lace or lace-trimmed table runners and place mats over blue denim tablecloths. Reverse the pattern by laying a lace tablecloth first and covering it with a lace-trimmed denim table runner or place mat. Add lace bow accents down the center of the denim table runner or to the side of the denim place mat. To increase the casual and formal decor contrast, set a pair of silver candelabra with long, white, elegant candle tapers down the center of each table. Set each place setting with fine china, crystal, and silverware. Add a lovely lace wedding-handkerchief napkin, tied with a denim ribbon, at each setting. This pattern can also be reversed using a denim napkin wrapped with a paper lace doily. Use a jar of home-canned pickles or apple butter as novel place cards. Top each jar with a lace doily laid over a circle of denim and tied with a pretty satin ribbon. Tie name cards to the ribbons or place a personalized label on each jar.

Treat guests to a down-home farm meal. Again, contrast the casual with the formal. Serve the meal family-style, placing bowls of food directly on the table. However, put the food on pretentious silver trays and in decorative crystal bowls. Try this farm fresh menu: thick baked pork chops; hot, steamy mashed farm potatoes; garden-grown succotash (corn and lima beans); tossed green salad with fresh garden vegetables; and home-baked bread served with hand-churned butter. Prepare a special denim and lace anniversary cake. Place a double-layer chocolate cocoa cake on a cake plate trimmed with a denim ruffle. Add a lacy powdered sugar design to the top of the cake. To make the lacy design, sprinkle powdered sugar over a paper doily, removing the doily after the dusting. After dinner, hold an old-fashioned square dance.

Anniversary Gift Suggestions

Present the couple with one of these lace treasures:

- Lace tablecloth, lace table runner, or set of lace place mats or napkins
- Copy of the movie *Arsenic and Old Lace*
- Bottle of wine glued with decorative lace appliqués
- Handmade lace tea-towel pillow
- Lace-appliquéd flowerpot filled with a garden bloom
- Imitation bear rug, matching pair of faux-fur ear muffs, an antique quilt, or his-and-her blue jeans (The modern anniversary gifts listed for the thirteenth anniversary are textiles and furs, which suggest a wide variety of gift ideas.)

A Special Moment for the Anniversary Couple

Send a Lacy Valentine

Will you be my Valentine? St. Valentine's Day is filled with frilly lace-trimmed chocolate heart boxes and lace heart valentines. Create anniversary valentine romance any time of the year. Send a different lacy valentine with a romantic sentiment every day for a month leading up to the anniversary day. On the day of your anniversary, substitute the daily valentine card with a large, lace-decorated chocolate candy heart box. Attach a note inviting your spouse to an evening laced with romance. Replace the heart-box chocolates with a lace teddy or nightgown—and enjoy the response.

The Fourteenth Anniversary
—Ivory—

Toast: To true love—rare and beautiful as ivory!

Just as the elephant and its beautiful ivory tusks deserve respect and admiration, so does a fourteen-year marriage. For years, ivory has been the traditional fourteenth anniversary designation. Unfortunately, worldwide demand for ivory has created a poaching industry that has endangered elephants. But important steps have been taken in recent years to prevent the slaughter of these magnificent beasts. Celebrate these ivory-themed anniversary parties by honoring the elephant along with the anniversary couple. After all, long marriages are themselves endangered species!

Big Top Anniversary Circus

Elephants remind us of Jumbo the elephant and the "Greatest Show on Earth"—the circus. Elephants lead a circus parade of clownin' around fun, monkeyshines, and carnival games. Gather friends and family for an "under the big top" anniversary celebration.

Invitation Ideas

Send a circus ticket to family and friends written on—or attached to—one of these expressions:

- Toy elephant
- Bag of peanuts
- Box of animal crackers
- Huge pair of brightly colored clown glasses
- Popcorn box
- Bouquet of brightly colored helium balloons (You can also write invitation details on an inflated balloon. Deflate it for mailing. Guests can blow the balloon up to read the invitation.)
- Taped recording of a circus barker calling out invitation details while perky circus music plays in the background
- Photo of the anniversary couple in elephant or clown costumes
- Box of Cracker Jack

Special Instructions for Guests

Send this ringmaster announcement: "Ladies and Gentleman! It's the ivory anniversary. Please bring a white-elephant gift (something of little or no value) for a carnival game exchange." You may also ask guests to come dressed in circus "party animal" costumes.

Decorating Touches

Transform the party area into a big top extravaganza.

- Greet guests from a ticket booth at the party entrance.
- Drape bright circus-colored cloth—or twist crepe paper streamers—from the center of the ceiling to create a big top canopy.
- Line the entryway with helium balloons secured from the floor, floating shoulder high.
- Hang circus and elephant posters trimmed with colorful balloons and swirled crepe paper streamers on the wall.
- Cover tables with brightly striped cloths and add a floating helium balloon to the back of each guest's chair.

- Circus acts take center stage. Place plush elephants, plush monkeys, giant clown shoes, or clown dolls in the center of a Hula-Hoop as table centerpieces. Attach crepe paper clown collars and helium balloon bouquets to the animals for added festivity.
- Place several cotton-candy-filled cones in a centerpiece stand made from a brightly painted box. Cut holes through the top of the box to support the cones.
- Make circus place cards, writing guests' names on one of the following items:
  —Ice cream cone with a small round balloon or carnation flower top
  —Box of Cracker Jack
  —Clown nose attached to a die-cut clown-face card
  —Plastic elephant nose
  —Bag of peanuts
  —Circus ticket replica
  —Box of animal crackers
  —Huge pair of brightly colored clown glasses
  —Ribbon-tied bag of cotton candy
  —Popcorn box
- In honor of Jumbo the elephant, decorate with Jumbo-sized popcorn boxes, clown cutouts, and balloons.

Theme-Inspired Activities and Entertainment

Here are some circus ring and midway entertainment ideas:

- Create a circus ring by painting a huge ring on the floor or by trimming a circled area with crepe paper or brightly painted cardboard boxes. If you have room, create a three-ring circus.
- Have a ringmaster of ceremonies lead friends and family in entertaining and death-defying circus acts:
  —Elephant tricks (Perform a line-dance routine dressed in gray padded sweatpants, a matching sweatshirt, a tail, and a long elephant trunk.)

—A high wire act (Dress toddlers in tutus and ballerina slippers and have them dance across a death-defying high wire—painted or chalked on the ground, of course.)

—Put a clown collar on Fido. Entertain the audience with a circus dog show, teaching Fido to jump through a Hula-Hoop and do other dog tricks.

—Bring out your cat and a licorice whip for a (gentle) lion-taming demonstration.

—The whole world loves a clown. "Send in the clowns" to the center ring for a temporary clown college. Have the professional clowns recruit some audience members and instruct them in the art of clown makeup, costumes, and clownin' around.

• Hire a pianist to tickle the ivories.

• Have circus vendors distribute circus treats to the crowd while yelling, "Popcorn, peanuts, cotton candy!"

• Conduct a circus parade of party animals (costumed guests).

• Set up some elephant-antics carnival games in the midway:

—Toss peanuts in glass goblets.

—Toss rings around plush elephant toys.

—Throw beanbags at plush elephant toys sitting on circus risers.

• Also in the midway, offer animal balloons and animal-face painting.

• Exchange the white-elephant gifts requested in the *Special Instructions for Guests* section. Pass the gifts around to the tune of circus music in a musical-chairs-like activity. Guests keep the gift they are holding when the music stops.

Menu Ideas

Serve carnival treats from concession stands. Build concession stand backdrops with Cracker Jack box pyramids and colorful candylike balloon towers. (Use large Life Saver candylike balloons.)

• Hot dogs on a stick

• French fries sprinkled with vinegar and served in cardboard tubs

• Elephant ears (a cinnamon and sugar-sprinkled fried carnival pastry dessert)

• Cotton candy and Sno-cones

- Ice cream cones and root beer floats
- Bright red candy apples and chewy caramel apples
- Popcorn and peanuts
- Freshly squeezed lemonade and Jumbo-sized, ice-cold sodas
- Clown ice cream cones (Turn an ice cream cone upside down on a cupcake paper. Decorate the ice cream ball with candy clown face decorations. Add icing buttons to the clown cone hat.)

Party Favors with Flair

Send guests home with a bag of circus goodies.
- Carnival game prizes
- Small toy elephants
- Box of Cracker Jack
- Bag of peanuts
- Box of animal crackers
- Huge pair of brightly colored clown glasses
- Bouquet of brightly colored helium balloons

Anniversary Safari

Ask guests to join you on a safari to tame the wild chocolate "beasty." They'll enjoy an evening of delectable chocolate treats among the sights and sounds of the African wildlife kingdom. Play wildlife sound recordings and cover the room with lots of green plants and trees. Rent the foliage from a florist, event decorator, or rental company. Hang safari-animal-print balloons and use them to build balloon towers and arches. Hide large, freestanding cutouts of elephants, zebras, lions, and giraffes. Provide a buffet table canopied with mosquito netting and label it "Rations Station." Drape the netting from the ceiling to the outside corners of the table. You'll also need to know where the watering hole is in this jungle climate, so attach a tent awning or thatched roof above the bar and hang a "Watering Hole" sign on it.

Cover tables with floor-length, ivory-colored tablecloths. Then top each table with animal-print cloths such as zebra, tiger, and leopard. Lay five oversized green felt leaves on the table, stretching them from the center to the edges. For the centerpiece, choose a camping lantern surrounded by green plants and a basket of fruit. Add chocolate candy bars to the fruit basket as chocolate safari accents. Also, place chocolate-dipped bottles of champagne at each table. Cover each bottle with plastic wrap before dipping. Guests can then peel away and nibble on the chocolate coating. For a novel place card statement, write the name of each guest on a banana.

Invite guests to this chocolate safari by gluing invitation details to African safari travel brochures. Ask each guest to bring something chocolate for a chocolate-concoctions buffet. Chocolate choices are plentiful: chocolate candy and cakes, chocolate-covered potato chips, chocolate cheese, chocolate coffee, and even chocolate-liqueur-filled goblets. Provide a wildly delicious chocolate anniversary cake. Don't forget to help offset all that sugar with cheese, fruit, and crudités trays.

Greet guests with plastic safari hats and toy binoculars from an "Expedition Check-In Station." Then lead guests on a safari adventure in which the only shooting going on involves instant cameras and video recorders. Divide safari passengers into groups, appointing a safari guide and distributing safari hunt lists. Award points for each listed safari sight recorded such as the following:

—Peel a chocolate kiss with animal claws (mittens decorated with felt animal claws).

—Catch as many party animals (guests) as possible in a Hula-Hoop.

—"Shoot" an animal trio song performance (one person performing a lion roar, a second person imitating a monkey screech, and a third person acting out an elephant cry).

—Find a dancing monkey and elephant (recruit whomever you can).

Show instant photos and videotapes of safari hunts later in the evening.

Hire an entertainment company to walk around with wild animals. Guests can pet monkeys and baby lions. It's even possible to bring in an alligator for a rare entertainment experience. (See the *Supplier Resource Directory*.) For more monkeying around, arrange for a costumed gorilla character to jump out from "jungle brush." Guests will go ape for the chocolate-covered frozen bananas he'll pass out.

Anniversary Gift Suggestions

Choose an ivory-inspired gift for the anniversary couple.

- Tickets to the circus to see the elephants
- Ivory-colored set of bed sheets
- Ivory-colored tablecloth
- Imitation ivory box
- Imitation ivory letter opener
- Elephant figurine
- Tickets to an "ivory keys" piano concert
- Matching gold necklaces, gold bracelets, or gold key chains engraved with the couple's names and fourteenth anniversary date (Gold jewelry is the modern fourteenth anniversary gift designation.)

A Special Moment for the Anniversary Couple

A Secluded Ivory Tower

Create an ivory tower just for the two of you. Hide away in a luxury hotel or quaint bed-and-breakfast for the weekend. If budget allows, go on a romantic African safari.

The Fifteenth Anniversary
—Crystal—

Toast: To the crystal clear love that you share for each other.

A beautiful marriage, like a crystal, is not formed overnight. After fifteen years, a marriage has had time to crystallize into a loving, confident, happy relationship. An anniversary such as this calls for a spectacular celebration among family and friends. Celebrate the couple's crystal clear love for each other with sparkling fun and romance.

A Crystal Carnival

Invite guests to a crystal ice palace of fun and romance in a winter wonderland.

Invitation Ideas

Insert an "Our love for one another is crystal clear" invitation into a snow white envelope. Then send it with one of these frosty accents:

- Crystal rock candy
- Glittering sugar cubes placed in a clear cellophane bag and tied with an iridescent ribbon

- Sparkling snowball (To make the snowball, glue imitation snow-flakes around a Styrofoam ball and spray it with opalescent glitter.)
- Small clear bag of crystal snow (Epsom salts).

Special Instructions for Guests

Make it a white-tie affair, asking guests to dress in all-white formalwear.

Decorating Touches

Create a crystal ice palace by transforming your party site into a winter wonderland.

For the Room
- Use all-white decorations.
- Illuminate the area with crystal-like sparkling lights.
- Set up a snow cave entrance. Make the passage with an arched tunnel of white iridescent balloons or a continuous tunnel of arch-shaped, scallop-edged curtains softly lit with ice blue lights. White vinyl icicle curtains could also be used to create a tunnel effect.
- Set the party up around an indoor ice rink.
- Cover a tabletop with mirror tiles before displaying name tags or table assignments. Add votive candles for sparkling reflections.
- Drape the walls with sheer white fabric. Use ice blue up-lighting against the walls and hang twinkle lights behind the fabric to create the illusion of a sparkling snow cave.
- Guests will walk into a dazzling crystal forest, a room encircled with white Christmas trees lit with ice blue or white twinkle lights. Sprinkle artificial snow at the trees' bases.
- Let it snow, let it snow, let it snow! Form imitation snow piles and create reflective frozen pond scenes using blue or silver Mylar paper. Add toy cold water friends to the arctic scenery such as furry, white sea pups, fluffy, white polar bears, and tuxedo-clad penguins.
- Decorate bar and food buffets to resemble igloos using blocks of white Styrofoam.
- Set each buffet with large, lighted, crystalline ice sculptures carved into romantic heart, lovebird, and wedding bell designs.

For Tables

Cover guest tables with festive and frosty accents.

- Use floor-length, opalescent cloths. Wrap matching chair covers with long, flowing tie sashes made with sheer iridescent fabric.
- Create glowing table icebergs. Shine a glowing ice blue light shining up through glass-topped guest tables covered with sheer white fabric.
- Set each place setting with crystal clear plates and crystal stemware. Wrap a light blue glow-in-the-dark stick around each plate.
- Wrap opalescent napkins with strings of imitation crystal beads.
- Sprinkle the entire table with imitation snow.
- Make a sparkling crystal centerpiece:

  —A mix-match of frosty snow glassware comes together beautifully. Cover several different glass goblets, candlesticks, and glass containers with crystal snow frost. Use a spray can of artificial snow or paint the glassware with a crystal-like slush mixture made from Epsom salts. Add just enough water to the Epsom salts to create a slightly wet salt mixture (about one tablespoon water to one cup Epsom salts, adding more water as needed). Using a paintbrush, decoratively brush the slush onto the glassware. Let each side begin to harden before turning. Then let the piece solidify for at least twenty-four hours before using. Dry Epsom salts can also be poured into goblets, globes, bowls, or vases to resemble snow.

  —Make crystal cellophane bouquets. Gather a bunch of fresh flowers together with a rubber band, flaring the stems out as supportive legs. Gather crystal clear cellophane up and around the stem base. Fill the cellophane with water before securing with another rubber band and tying with a decorative bow.

  —Place several crystal decanters and crystal candlestick holders along with tall, white taper candles on a large mirror tile to create a romantic sparkling centerpiece.

  —Showcase a crystal figurine on a mirror tile with reflective candlelight accents.

  —Float white candles and silver metallic or white iridescent confetti in a bowl or goblet grouping filled with crystal clear water.

Theme-Inspired Activities and Entertainment

Capture the festive crystal carnival spirit with this flurry of winter fun:

- Meet guests with Eskimo-costumed greeters. Offer instant photo opportunities with the greeters and their snow white Siberian-husky-led dogsled.

- Have entertainers dressed in all-white costumes mingle with guests. Hire a selection of crystal carnival entertainers including a pirouette mime, juggler, carnival barker, stilt-walker, and clown to greet and mingle with guests. Make sure all the entertainers' accessories and props (balls, balloons, and so on) are white colored, too.

- Set up snow white carnival booths, tents, or awnings around the perimeter of the room. Dress booth attendants in white costumes and stock the booths with snow white and crystal prizes such as white teddy bears, white ear muffs or stocking caps, crystal-like jewelry, and small crystal figurines or bowls.

  —Toss dimes into crystal (sturdy glass) goblets.

  —Arm party guests with Styrofoam "snow balls" to throw through white-painted, hanging tires.

  —Throw darts at snow white prize balloons.

  —Set up a plush-animal-toss game. Throw a hoop over a snow white plush animal toy and its square base to win the toy.

  —Add a "floating ducks" booth using clear- or white-painted plastic ducks.

- Offer crystal ball fortunetelling from a snow white tent. The snow queen fortuneteller could also pass out fortunes kept in a crystal bowl.

- Invite guests to dance to a live band or DJ under a revolving crystal mirror ball.

- Stage a "crystal" toast to the anniversary couple and welcome guests to the evening's celebration. Ask guests to play the carnival games, enjoy the food buffets, and delight in libations and conversation throughout the affair.

Menu Ideas

As part of the event décor and ambiance, set up vendor carts around the room serving snow-colored treats such as white-chocolate candy apples, white cotton candy, hot white chocolate, popcorn, and vanilla ice cream. Later in the evening, ring a crystal bell to announce a lavish spread of ice-palace opulence:

- Pass hot hors d'oeuvres, such as wild mushrooms in puff pastry and scallops wrapped in bacon, using silver-tray service.
- Serve sparkling champagne in crystal stemware from an attention-getting silver fountain.
- Set up carving stations for roasted prime rib of beef miniroll sandwiches with horseradish and gourmet mustards. Add another station for whole-roasted turkey miniroll sandwiches with cranberry chutney and gourmet mustard.
- Add a display of domestic and international cheeses, garnished with fresh French bread, wafers, and crackers.
- Set up another presentation of fresh garden vegetables, sliced seasonal fruits, and berries placed in crystal ice bowls. Add the chef's specialty sauces for each.
- Instead of traditional anniversary cake, serve a flaming Baked Alaska with its magnificent snowlike peaks.

Party Favors with Flair

Offer each guest a sparkling party favor gift at each place setting or distribute gifts from a crystal carnival vendor cart.

- Small crystal ornament wrapped in crystal cellophane (Choose a crystal medallion commemorating the couple's anniversary, a crystal rose, or a small crystal animal or figure.)
- Crystal charm hung on ribbon
- Crystal prism
- Cellophane bag filled with snowball cookies—round powdered sugar cookies commonly referred to as Mexican Wedding Cakes or Russian Tea Cakes (Tie the bag with a sparkling iridescent bow.)

Glass Slipper Ball

The anniversary couple's Cinderella glass slipper dream will come true with this party. Celebrate with grand and royal finesse this once-upon-a-time fairy tale. With the help of fairy godmother magic, guests will experience exquisite Renaissance splendor.

Send a small glass slipper with a scroll invitation. Find small glass (plastic) slippers in the favor section of party supply or craft stores. Ask guests to come dressed in Renaissance period ballroom costumes. The handsome prince and his Cinderella princess—the royal anniversary couple—should also dress in Renaissance finery. Line up the royal couple, in their sparkling tiara and royal crown, alongside their royal family members for a majestic reception line. Guests will be greeted after walking down a long red carpet runway lined with crystal clocks (all set to twelve midnight) placed on ivy-wrapped gold columns. Then they'll follow the red carpet through an archway created by shiny swords held by the Royal Army.

At the other end of the sword tunnel, guests will be met with a ballroom covered in royal purple and gold Renaissance splendor. Hang royal banners from the ceiling and canopy the head table with the same majestic pageantry. Drape each guest table in a gold lamé or purple velvet, floor-length cloth. Decorate tables with glass slipper centerpieces. Place glasslike slippers on red velvet pillows trimmed with gold braid and tassels. Department stores and bridal shops sometimes carry a clear, high-heeled shoe. Also, jewelry and gift stores occasionally carry a miniature crystal shoe. If these are unavailable, make a glass slipper by covering a white, high-heeled shoe with iridescent beading or sequins. Use gold-dusted (lightly sprayed) miniature pumpkins as novel place cards. Tie each with a place card attached to a sheer white- and gold-trimmed ribbon. Evoke the romantic Cinderella fantasy by having a florist or decorator make a room centerpiece such as a sparkling-lights-covered pumpkin coach or glass-slipper wire sculpture.

Set the Renaissance mood with a hammer-dulcimer musician. Announce the start of the royal feast with a Renaissance-clad musician blowing a clarion (a long, straight medieval trumpet) or other modern day horn. Preset crystal ice bowls of salad at each place setting to start the extravagant crystal ball menu. (Make ice bowls by freezing lemon and herb spring water between two concentric bowls. While freezing, weight the top bowl with a can of vegetables.) Ceremoniously announce and parade each course with the sound of the clarion and pomp-and-circumstance music. Serve a royal banquet of crystal clear consommé, Cornish game hens, roast pig, roast leg of lamb with mint jelly, medleys of assorted new potatoes and hot steaming vegetables, stone-ground bread, and slipper-shaped pats of butter.

During dinner, entertain guests with fairy godmother, magic wand charm—a Cinderella marionette show. After dinner, provide a grand orchestra for ballroom dancing and anniversary festivities. Choose a castle-shaped anniversary cake or a magnificent tiered creation topped with a sugar-made glass slipper. Frame the cake table with large glass-slipper ice sculptures surrounded by pyramids of crystal champagne goblets. Cut the cake with a shiny ceremonial sword and serve each piece with a flaming scoop of brandied ice cream. Toast the anniversary couple with pewter goblets filled with mead, a type of honey wine dating back to the Middle Ages. Engrave the champagne goblets with the couple's names and anniversary date as take-home party favors. End this storybook anniversary party with happily-ever-after pumpkin coach rides. (See the *Supplier Resource Directory*.)

Anniversary Gift Suggestions

Choose a sparkling piece of crystal as the fifteenth anniversary gift.

- Crystal bowl, vase, or pair of candlesticks
- Cut-crystal set of wine or champagne goblets
- Crystal figurine or dinner bell
- Crystal photo frame
- Crystal anniversary clock (a crystal-domed clock that is set and wound once a year on the designated anniversary date)
- Antique crystal candelabrum
- Crystal chandelier
- Crystal punch bowl
- Crystal cake plate
- Crystal heart pendant, key chain, tie tack, or cuff links
- The crystal sparkle of Dom Perignon, perfect for putting a sparkle in your sweetheart's eye
- His-and-her monogrammed watches, a subscription to *Time* magazine, a copy of the movie *Somewhere in Time*, or a book on time

management (These "time for love" gift suggestions are inspired by the modern gift designation for the fifteenth wedding anniversary—watches.)

A Special Moment for the Anniversary Couple

Crystal Pool Reflection

Recover from all the sparkling fun of the evening by booking the next night in a hotel room just for the two of you. Choose a hotel that offers a private pool or large Jacuzzi in your room. Line the pool or tub with crystal candlestick holders placed on small mirror tiles to reflect the sparkling candlelight. Arrange for room service to deliver sparkling champagne and strawberries. Then immerse yourselves in the soothing water.

Crystal Champagne Sunrise Toast

Create a memorable crystal memory just for the two of you. Greet the dawn with a special champagne toast. Pour sparkling champagne into crystal goblets and snuggle up together on a beach or inside in front of a large picture window to watch the dazzling sunrise.

The Sixteenth through Nineteenth Anniversaries —Sweet Imaginations—

Toast: To imaginative romance and
a marriage of loving and dreamy diversions!

Anniversary lists don't detail particular gifts or designations for anniversaries sixteen through nineteen. However, every anniversary is a time to celebrate, and a special affair can be assembled with a little imagination. Dream up a special party for these in-between years or choose one of the following anniversary creations.

"Sweet Sixteen" Sweetheart Affair

Envision a sentimental affair for the "sweet sixteen" (or seventeen, eighteen, or nineteen) anniversary sweethearts.

Invitation Ideas

Invite guests to this "sweet sixteen" sweetheart affair with one of the following sugary sentiments:

- Fill a small treat bag with sugar cubes or candy.
- Attach details to a package of Sweet Tart candies, an old-fashioned swirl-design lollipop, or a small box of chocolates.
- Send a handwritten note, sweet scented with perfume and a love poem.
- Write details on a piece of decorative paper cut into a heart shape and trimmed with lace or a paper doily. In its center, paste a photo of the anniversary sweethearts or a copy of this Helen Keller poem:

> *The best and most beautiful things in the world*
> *cannot be seen or even touched.*
> *They must be felt with the heart.*

- Write invitation details on the back of a child's valentine card, adding some candy conversation hearts to the envelope. Or, place an engraved invitation inside an empty, heart-shaped, and elaborately decorated valentine chocolates box.
- Send a sweet pea or sweet William flower seed packet or note card.
- Attach an invitation label to a sweet basil spice jar.
- Send a printed invitation inside a heart-shaped photo frame.
- Write invitation details directly on a small heart-shaped pillow.
- Write details on the back of a love-letter-inscribed envelope tied with a pretty ribbon.
- Superimpose the anniversary couple's photographed faces over the King and Queen of Hearts playing cards. Send the two cards, tied together with a pretty red ribbon, with the invitation.

Special Instructions for Guests

Enclose a special paper and heart-shaped lace doily for guests to write a straight-from-the-heart anniversary wish for the anniversary couple.

Decorating Touches

Cover the party area with romantic, heartwarming décor.

For the Room

- Fill the room with heart-shaped balloons.
- Add an "Anniversary Sweethearts" congratulatory banner.
- Line the walls with heart-framed photos of the anniversary couple. For a fun, nostalgic touch, include a few of their childhood photos as well.
- Decorate a photo-op area with a balloon heart arch. Take instant photos of guests with their sweethearts.
- Decorate winter climate yards with birdseed hearts described below in the *Theme-Inspired Activities and Entertainment* section.

For the Tables

- The tables will look "pretty in pink" with sweetheart pink cloths and white or gold cane chairs, covered with sheer white organza material and two large pink sash bows. Choose white organza-wrapped crystal vases, filled with pink roses, to grace the center of the tables. Or, go with a huge heart-shaped pink helium balloon, tethered to a hot air balloon basket filled with pink carnations.
- Blanket the entire top of a white-clothed table with the sweet fragrance of sumptuous red roses (flower blooms floating in low, closely placed crystal containers) and soft-glowing votive candles.
- Float sweet-nothing sayings over tables with sheer white organza tablecloths inscribed with these gold-ink words or phrases: sweetie pie, honey, sugar, darling, love-ums, and so on. Add gold-painted flowerpot centerpieces filled with sweet pea and sweet Willliam plants.
- Cover the tables with smoldering red tablecloths and matching chair covers. Add fiery centerpiece candle groupings burning in crystal stemware and placed on reflective mirror tiles. Fill various-height stemware pieces with tiny red-hot candies and watch the candy confections melt with sizzling romance.

- Add some heart-beating table accents:
—Heart-shaped doily placed under each plate
—Heart-shaped folded napkin laid across each dinner plate
—Valentine or ribbon-tied love letter left at each place setting
—Candy conversation hearts or shiny red confetti heart accents scattered across the table
—Sweet talk message napkins or gold-ribbon-tied cards written with gold ink messages such as sweetie pie, honey, sugar, darling, love-ums, and so on
—Dinner plates set inside the bottom half of an empty, heart-shaped valentine chocolates box (Use the ribbon- and flower-decorated top halves in a table centerpiece arrangement.)
- Make a unique place card statement writing guests' names on one of these sweet items:
—Decorative teacup filled with sugar cubes
—Ribbon-tied package of Sweet Tarts or a small box of chocolates
—Old-fashioned swirl-design lollipop
—Cellophane bag filled with sugar cubes or candy conversation hearts tied with a lovely satin bow
—Sweet pea or sweet William flower seed packet or note card
—Labeled sweet basil spice jar
—Heart-shaped photo frame
—Sweetheart rose with an attached romantic verse and message reading, "A sweet sentiment picked just for you"
—Small heart-shaped pillow

Theme-Inspired Activities and Entertainment

Inspire guests' imaginations with sweet and romantic pastimes.
- Ask guests to come dressed as a famous heartthrob celebrity.
- Randomly assign a "world's greatest sweetheart" name tag to guests as they arrive. Examples include Romeo, Juliet, Cleopatra, Antony, Rhett, Scarlett, and so on. Instruct guests to find their corresponding sweetheart dinner partners.

- Assign this childhood-sweethearts activity: Ask guests to bring a baby picture of themselves to the party. Gather photos and randomly distribute female photos to male guests and vice versa. Guests must then figure out whose pictures they have and sit with those persons at dinner.

- Leave sweetheart messages for the birds in snow-climate areas: Have guests use a stick to draw heart outlines in the snow. Then have them pat the snow down firmly and fill it with birdseed, nuts, and berries.

- Collect the title of each couple's special song as they arrive at the party. Then have the band or orchestra play a medley of "our songs" throughout the evening.

- Conduct a heartfelt toast and ask guests to share their straight-from-the-heart anniversary wishes (requested in the invitations) with the anniversary couple.

- Hold a "Sweetie Pie" auction to benefit the couple's favorite charity. Beforehand, ask each guest to bring a pie for auctioning. Then have a professional auctioneer or volunteer MC conduct a live auction.

- Enjoy a card game of Hearts.

Menu Ideas

Win guests' hearts with these sweetheart menu items. Mix and match your choices to create a from-the-heart menu:

- His-and-her beef or ham steaks
- Hearth-cooked eye-of-round roast (See the *Theme-Inspired Activities and Entertainment* section in "The Seventh Anniversary: Wool and Copper" chapter.)
- Sweetie pot pies (chicken and beef)
- Sweet vegetable delights from the heartland of America including sweet peas, sweet peppers, sweet potatoes, and sweet corn
- Heart-shaped home fries (Use a small cookie cutter.)
- Sweetheart Jell-O mold
- Sweet basil bread
- Steaming heart-shaped rolls, biscuits, and cornbread
- Hearty breakfast items such as heart-shaped pancakes, sausage, and eggs (Hint: Use a large metal cookie cutter to form pancakes and eggs into heart shapes right in the skillet.)

- Sweet-and-sour shrimp, chicken, and pork dishes
- "Have a heart" shaped pizzas
- Sweet-talking iced sugar cookies (Write a candy-conversation-heart message on each cookie.)
- Chocolate sweet-tooth dessert buffet filled with a glorious assortment of tantalizing chocolate (chocolate cheesecake, chocolate-dipped spoons, chocolate-rimmed glasses filled with liqueur, truffle-bedecked topiaries, heart-shaped triple-chocolate brownies, sponge cake drizzled with chocolate hazelnut spread, and more)

Party Favors with Flair

Get to the heart of each guest with a sweet memento:

- Candy box tied with a sweet-nothings sentiment such as sweetie pie, honey, sugar, darling, love-ums, and so on
- Lace pouch filled with sweet-smelling potpourri
- Ribbon-tied cellophane bag of sweetmeats (sweet candy concoctions)
- Heart charm
- Small photo of the sweetheart anniversary couple placed in a heart-shaped frame
- One gloriously perfect sweetheart rose
- Sweet sentiment written on a white linen card with a gold pen and tied with a gold ribbon

Happy Seventeenth: The Art of Romance

For the seventeenth anniversary, imagine a party masterpiece painted with colorful expression. This work-of-art party could also be enjoyed on the other in-between anniversary years. Start by creating a special art exhibit, showcasing some of the master impressionists: Vincent Van Gogh, Claude Monet, Paul Cézanne, and Henri Matisse. Hang various prints of these European masters throughout the room. Paint each guest table with a different color or use colored tablecloths, each color representing a different artist's work.

Cover a Monet table with a water blue tablecloth accented with rainbow-colored napkins. Add a water lily centerpiece, using one of Monet's favorite subjects. Decorate another table with a fierce-colored tablecloth color like the intense blue from Van Gogh's *Starry Night* or the passionate yellow from his *Sunflowers*. Add coordinating napkin colors and bring the table to life with centerpieces that were the Dutch painter's two favorite subjects: iris and sunflower blossoms. Create another "objet d'art" centerpiece using Paul Cézanne's *Still Life with Apples* as the subject. Drape the table with either a neutral-colored canvas material or mint green tablecloth. Place a white china plate piled with red and golden apples at the center of the table. Finally, create a vivid table inspired by Henry Mattise's *Woman with the Hat*. Brush the table with a deep green tablecloth stroked with bold napkins in blue, red, yellow, and black. Add a large, elaborate turn-of-the-century lady's hat to the center of the table.

For all the tables, cut painter's palette shapes from foam board or poster board to use as novel napkin holders. Set a post card or note card copy of the painter's work on a small easel and inscribe each as individual place cards. Pass out seating assignments attached to a painter's brush (this would also make a unique invitation statement) or paint invitation details on canvas. During the party, have local artists or caricaturists sketch drawings of the guests. Provide a painter's smock (canvas aprons imprinted with museum art) and sets of oil-paint favors for guests to use in creating their masterpieces. Serve a menu filled with delectable colors: chicken cordon *bleu*, *orange*-glazed carrots, fresh salad *greens*, new *red* potatoes, and fresh, steaming *brown* bread. For dessert, create a special anniversary cake buffet serving an assortment of European masterpieces: German chocolate cake, French chocolate chestnut torte, English sponge cake, and Italian Zuppa Inglese (an elaborately decorated rum cake).

An Eighteen "Hole" Years Anniversary Golf Championship

Take a swing at celebrating eighteen "hole" years of married life with this anniversary party. You can also customize your "golf course" design to other anniversary years. Paste invitations, including your party tee time, to a copy of *Golf Illustrated* or place your invitation in a golf ball box along with a golf ball. Contact your local golf course or sporting goods store for empty boxes.

Invite serious golf enthusiasts to a "putt and party" complete with various golf course challenges: a driving cage, putting greens, a chip shot practice area, golf video games and virtual reality simulators, and on-site professional instructors. Or, set up a special anniversary tee time in the morning and hold a golf-themed luncheon afterward.

To create a just-for-fun golf party, take guests to a miniature golf course or create a backyard or indoor course. Lay out a course complete with water hazards, traps, and tunnels. Purchase tin putting cups from a sporting goods store or golf pro shop. Decorate each hole with a memento representing a time in the couple's life. Ideas might include a baby-doll obstacle (include photos of the children) to represent the births of their children. Place a bowl of water at the bottom of a ramp to represent a special lake vacation. Or, encourage some on-the-greens putting-hole design. Separate golfers into foursomes to compete in a decorating contest. Provide each group with play money to purchase artificial turf, cardboard, cups, and miscellaneous decorations from the party's pro shop. Each hole must be decorated with a par-for-the-course anniversary theme. Award a prize for the most creative design. Award prizes for other "not-so-traditional" golf contests as well: the longest drive with a marshmallow, the best karaoke foursome, the most creative foursome photo pose, and so on. Award golf books or anniversary-monogrammed golf towels as prizes.

Cover dining tables with felt, putting-green tablecloths, centered with a hole-in-one cup and flag number. Or, use a bucket of golf balls as a dual centerpiece and party activity. Number each ball beforehand for a lottery prize. Use golf towels as napkins and scorecards as unique place cards. Park several golf carts off to the side, tied with "Happy Anniversary!" helium balloon bouquets.

Have bartenders dress in old-fashioned caddie costumes and serve drinks from behind an artificial-turf-covered bar. Then roll out a golf-course food and beverage cart to serve guests championship party snacks including "country club" sandwiches, hole-in-one bagel pizzas, "chip shots" (potato chips) and dip, putting-green salad, and iced "tee." Send guests home with a special tee-time favor such as a tea bag decorated with golf tees, a teacup filled with golf tees, golf ball truffles, or a golf-tee-decorated frame filled with an instant photo of each guest with the anniversary twosome.

"Cloud Nineteen": An Angelic Affair

Guests will be on "cloud nineteen" with this angelic affair. Invite guests by sending an angel kiss (Hershey's Kiss) with a note reading, "A marriage kissed by an angel." Or, you could invite guests by sending a scroll, wrapped with a lovely white ribbon and feather, that reads, "Bill and Judy—A love touched by the whisper of an angel's wing."

Have angel-costumed greeters welcome guests at an elaborate pearly gate entrance to a splendid cloud-like room. Float gold balloons about for a streets-of-gold entryway. Line the walls with sky blue and cloud white murals. Float angel-shaped and angel-designed balloons on clouds of pearlescent balloons levitating near the ceiling. Wrap white Romanesque columns with sheer white tulle. Drape this same angel-wing-like material from the ceiling over strings of sparkling starlights. Perch angel-costumed actors, holding handheld harps, on cloud or pillar facades throughout the room.

Direct guests to seating assignments attached to a cloudlike bag or cone of cotton candy labeled Cloud #1, Cloud #2, and so on. Drape tables with pure white cloths and accent them with sky blue napkins. Or, make delightful napkins by tying tie lace hankies into angel shapes. Construct chair-back angel wings (using white ostrich feathers or a feather boa) and gold-wire halos for the backs of white or gold lamé chair covers. You can also find angelic costume attire at costume shops and in gift catalogs. Add gold or white dinnerware with sparkling crystal or gold stemware to this "cloud nineteen" table scene. Next, center each heavenly table creation with elegant angel figurines or decorations placed on a cloud of cotton batting or decorating material. Position a tiny, ribbon-tied gold bell at each place setting with a note reading, "Ring to inspire an angel's kiss."

Serve a heavenly menu filled with angelic selections including heavenly tasting truffle soup, angel-light salmon soufflé, clouds of whipped potatoes, cherub-chubby ham steaks, string-bean halos (French green beans tied into a ring shape with won ton dough), fruit ambrosia, and an anniversary angel food cake covered with clouds of whipped cream.

Entertain guests before dinner with the angelic sounds of a golden harp. After dinner, waltz on the clouds (a fog-machine-enhanced dance floor) accompanied by an orchestra playing romantic music. Send guests home with ribbon-wrapped cellophane bags filled with angel food cake, meringue clouds, divinity fudge, or angel tree ornaments.

If you're in a snowflake climate and time of year, encourage the really spirited guests to enjoy some snow-angel-making fun. Guests lie in the snow and fan their legs together while moving their arms up and down to pack the snow in an angel shape.

Anniversary Gift Suggestions

Present a sweet imagination anniversary gift with heart, art, golf, or angelic appeal.

- Matching dream journals to record the couple's dreams
- Dream pillows (small scented pillows), a relaxation sleep machine, a relaxation tape with sounds of nature, or dreamy lingerie
- Heart-shaped music box, a heart-shaped Christmas tree ornament, or a decorative heart-shaped pillow
- Heart-shaped gift basket filled with sweet "scentiments": fragrant toiletries, aromatherapy candles, potpourri, and a romantic interludes CD or cassette
- Bouquet of sweetheart roses or a tussie-mussie (a small Victorian bouquet filled with sweet flower sentiments, with each flower representing a special meaning)
- Framed art prints of the masters or a year's membership for two at an art museum
- Bouquet of irises or sunflowers inspired by Van Gogh's works
- Commissioned oil painting of the anniversary couple
- Matching set of golf clubs, his-and-her golf shirts or sweaters, or a professional golf lesson gift certificate
- Angel figurines, handcrafted decorations, or Christmas tree ornaments
- Monthly subscription to heavenly desserts or fudge from a mail order bakery
- Valentine, art, golf, or angel coffee table book

A Special Moment for the Anniversary Couple

Sweet Imaginations

Blindfold your spouse with a satin cloth. Set the atmosphere with a wind-song nature tape and lie back on a cottony soft cloud of pillows. Test your loved one's senses with morsels of sweetness: strawberries and whipped cream, chocolate truffles, and sips of nose-tickling champagne. Then ask him or her to identify various aromas: the scent of a rose, the bouquet of a wine, and the smell of a spice or vanilla fragrance. Then share your dreams with one another, recording them in a special keepsake journal.

The Twentieth Anniversary
—China—

*Toast: Like sentimental china, "to love and to cherish,
to have and to hold,"
wedding vows grow more precious
as each year unfolds.*
—Inspired by a poem written by Helen Marie Zell

A twenty-year anniversary is sentimental, like heirloom china passed down from generation to generation. After twenty years of marriage, the couple knows the precious meaning behind their delicate, chinalike wedding vows. This anniversary is a time for celebrating sentimentality.

Roaring Twenties Anniversary Speakeasy

For this twenty-year anniversary, take a nostalgic trip back to the roaring 1920s. The twenties was a time when hemlines were rising, the Charleston was the craze, and speakeasies rebelled against prohibition.

Invitation Ideas

Invite guests to a roaring twenties anniversary speakeasy in your own red velvet room. Send this secret message to guests: "Pssst! The password to gain entrance to the secret hideaway is L-O-V-E." Attach the message to one of the following unique flapper era items:

• Long-handled cigarette holder
• Bottle of "hooch"
• Photo of the guests-of-honor dressed in 1920s costumes
• Record or album cover from the 1920s
• Newspaper reproduction from the era with an anniversary headline
• Private-label bottle of champagne

Special Instructions for Guests

Suggest that guests dress in twenties era costumes—flapper dresses and zoot suits.

Decorating Touches

Transform a basement recreation room or party area into the "Red Velvet Room" with red-velvet-draped walls and these decorating touches:

• Hang elaborate gold mirrors and twenties era paintings on the walls.
• Add 1920s art deco and antique knickknacks to the room.
• Make a "bathtub gin" room centerpiece. Fill an old-time claw-foot bathtub with ice and bottles of gin for making classic martinis—the stylish drink of the twenties. Also, as a hospitable gesture, add soda pop and a variety of "hooch," "snugglepup," "giggle water," and "red ink" (twenties era names for liquor, brews, and wine).
• Have gangster bouncers, complete with toy machine guns, check out arriving guests from behind a peephole in the door.
• Cover cocktail tables with white linen cloths. Top each table with a brandy snifter filled with a floating gardenia and illuminated by romantic tea candles.
• Attach place cards to a long-handled cigarette holder or cigar.
• Drape feather boas over the back of each chair.

Theme-Inspired Activities and Entertainment

Provide an atmosphere of all-out roaring twenties fun.

- Give guests Charleston lessons and dance to the music of the jazz age.
- Stage an FBI raid to bring in "suspects" for an instant photo session around the anniversary cake.
- Hold a martini and cigar tasting. Have tuxedo-clad waiters distribute them from silver trays.
- Run a private screening of the black-and-white film *The Roaring Twenties*.
- Direct and videotape on site your own roaring twenties anniversary movie.

Menu Ideas

Serve a roaring twenties midnight breakfast buffet.

- Stacks of *flapper*-jack pancakes served with fresh butter and "red ink" syrup
- Gangster-sized portions of scrambled eggs and melted cheese
- Strings of Tommy-gun sausage links (display with a toy machine gun)
- Charleston coffee cake
- Roaring fruit flambé
- Orange juice martinis
- "Al-Capone-a-chinos" (cappuccinos)

Party Favors with Flair

Send guests home with an anniversary speakeasy memento.

- "Hooch" bottle filled with candy
- China-framed photo of the guests-of-honor dressed in 1920s costumes
- Private-label bottle of champagne

China and Champagne Supper

Set out your best china and serve a champagne supper. Have a florist make a beautiful flower arrangement in a china bowl. Add china candlesticks, china bowls, and china serving plates. If you don't have enough of one china pattern, don't worry—it's chic to mix and match.

Invite guests with a pretty, inexpensive china plate picked up from your local second-hand store. Take a permanent-marking pen and write invitation details directly on each plate. Pack them securely with a handwritten note asking guests to bring a special memory of time shared with the anniversary couple. At the dinner, have each guest share his or her memory during a sentimental journey over dessert.

China Rose— The Perfume of Love

The China rose (a bloom from a number of garden rose varieties derived from the shrubbery Chinese rose) fills a room with the perfume of love. Invite guests to a romantic candlelight anniversary dinner with a perfume-scented note attached to a bottle of rose perfume. Lead guests on a rose-petal path to a dining room scented with China rose arrangements. Hang Chinese art on the walls. Set the table with rose-patterned china and sparkling crystal over crisp white linen. Add black-lacquered chairs for a dramatic Asian touch. Cover the entire table and floor with rose petals. Illuminate a collection of antique perfume bottles in the center of the table with tall, slender taper candles. Set a crystal bottle of rose perfume, tied with a small place card, for each guest. In addition, lay a single rose made of china with a Chinese-lettered note across each plate.

Serve a meal inspired by the beauty of roses. Start with a choice of won ton or sweet-and-sour soup served in china bowls. Serve a main course of rosemary chicken and mashed potatoes piped into rose-bloom shapes. Add flower-stem asparagus. For dessert, serve rose-petal anniversary cake and rose tea in Chinese teacups.

Anniversary Gift Suggestions

Here are some china-inspired twentieth anniversary gift ideas:

- China teapot with sugar and creamer service
- Chinese teapot and teacups
- Mix-match set of antique china teacups
- Missing piece or broken-piece replacement of the couple's formal or everyday china set
- China vase, picture frame, or figurine
- Gift certificate to a Chinese restaurant
- China cake plate presented with a special twentieth anniversary cake
- Set of china place cards
- Decorative, antique, china-plate wall hanging
- China clock
- China cabinet
- Platinum plate inscribed with the couple's names and the twentieth anniversary theme and date (The modern twentieth anniversary gift designation is platinum.)

A Special Moment for the Anniversary Couple

A China Picnic

Love is in the air with this romantic china picnic for two. Pack a picnic hamper with china plates, a china vase filled with fresh flowers, and Chinese takeout or a specially catered lunch. Drive to a park, the country, or the mountains. Spend a special moment flying a Chinese kite. Stop every now and then to share tea for two. Sip Chinese tea (kept warm in Thermoses) from china teacups.

The Twenty-Fifth Anniversary
—Silver—

Toast: To sterling silver love:
Grow old along with me! The best is yet to be . . .
—Inspired by a poem by Robert Browning

Known in the late nineteenth century as the "Silver Wedding," the twenty-fifth wedding anniversary called for a silver-accented reenactment of the ceremony down to its smallest details. Over the years, renewing wedding vows, recreating original wedding details, and decorating with silver have continued to be favorite twenty-fifth anniversary traditions. Enjoy one of these formal silver anniversary celebrations or accent a more casual anniversary party with silver charm.

A Traditional Silver Wedding Jubilee

Like the original wedding, the traditional silver anniversary is a memorable formal affair where the couple can publicly declare their love for each other once again. Many couples choose to repeat their wedding vows and duplicate the original cake, flowers, and decorations. Some even wear their original wedding clothes.

Invitation Ideas

Choose a formal invitation engraved with silver ink for this special occasion. Invitations engraved on a silverlike platter would also make a dramatic statement. (See the *Supplier Resource Directory.*) A model invitation looks like this:

```
1976—2001
The pleasure of your company is requested at
the Silver Wedding Jubilee
of
Mr. and Mrs. Darryl Lapp
Saturday, the nineteenth of December
at seven o' clock
308 Carr Street
Jackson, Michigan
```

Special Instructions for Guests

Enclose a handwritten note asking guests to bring a silver-lined memory to share about the couple.

Decorating Touches

Look through old wedding photos and scrapbooks to recreate some original wedding splendor. Make copies of appropriate photos to help the baker make a replica of the original wedding cake and the florist recreate the bridal bouquet, corsages, and floral arrangements. Then create an unmistakable air of silver wedding romance with these silver touches:

Silver Room Inspiration

- Hang an enlarged photo of the anniversary couple in a silver-colored frame. Choose either a wedding photo or current photo, or use both.

- Decorate the party area with poster-sized photo blowups of the couple and their family over the years including the couple's childhood photos. Drape crepe paper between photos with "25" silver cutout decorations.
- Wrap the bar with a long strip of metallic silver paper.
- Create a photo collage of the couple over the years.
- Design a silver royal haven for the anniversary couple as described in the Introduction (page xvii).

Silver Table Accents

- Make a lovely tablecloth statement using a silver-paint pen to write "I love you" along the edges of a white organza tablecloth.
- Make silvery moon tablecloths and matching napkins. Dip a potato-cut stencil or rubber stamp half-crescent-moon shape in silver paint to create stencil designs on a white or blue tablecloth. Hearts or the couple's initials also make romantic stencil designs.
- Try one of these silver creation centerpiece ideas:
  —Love abounds in passion red. Place twenty-five red roses in a silver vase.
  —Wrap the bases of silver candelabra with sheer white tulle.
  —Wrap several white candle tapers together using silver, nonflammable ribbon or cording. (Hint: Do not burn candles past the ribbon.) Set this arrangement with florist's clay in a silver bowl. Conceal the clay with piles of silver tree ornament balls and randomly draped silver bead garlands.
  —Place silver-painted fruit on a silver or crystal cake stand. Spray-paint the fruit lightly, letting its true color show through in places, and trim the arrangement with green ivy accents.
  —Fill silver ice buckets with flowers, silver tree ornament balls, or a topiary arrangement.
  —Wrap champagne bottles with metallic silver gift-wrap and tie with silver helium balloons.
  —Place arrangements of silver photo frames, containing photos of the anniversary couple and their family, in the center of the table.
  —Use a silver teapot or service as a unique flower vase.
  —Encircle bowls of fruit or other menu items with a swirl of organza printed with silver stars. Spray fabric with star designs using paper-star templates.

—Fill an antique silver-hinged jewelry box with a white rose floral arrangement.

- Accent each place setting with a little silver magic:
  —Trim napkins with silver cording, ribbon, or jingle bells.
  —Drape a swirl of silver bead garland over a folded napkin.
  —Wrap each napkin with a silver-sprayed leaf attached to a wire.
  —Tie napkins with wide metallic or sheer silver ribbons.
  —Place a silver candle in a wineglass at each place setting. Secure a taper candle in a wine stemware glass with florist's clay. Then fill the glass half-full with silver beads or marbles. Tie a silver ribbon around the rim of the glass.
  —Place a silver doily under each dinner plate.
  —Fold a silver doily over a triangle napkin fold and top it with a flower bloom.

- Leave a silver party favor for each guest:
  —Place a tiny silver bell kiss-a-gram at each place setting. Using thin silver ribbon, tie a note to each bell reading, "Ring to inspire a Silver Wedding kiss."
  —Place silver English cracker favors (decorative tubes containing small prizes) at each place setting. Purchase crackers commercially or make your own. Wrap cardboard tubes (filled with sweets, mottoes, or small favors) with tissue paper and tie the ends with a pretty ribbon. Then roll and paste a silver doily around each tube.
  —Leave a silver table-talk mixer card on each guest's plate. Using a silver-ink pen, write a milestone event from the year the couple was married on a small card. Tie each card with a sheer silver ribbon.

Theme-Inspired Activities and Entertainment

If possible, invite members of the original wedding party to stand with the anniversary couple as they repeat their vows. New vows can also be created especially for the silver anniversary. If possible, share vows in front of the original wedding officiant, accompanied by original or new wedding music.

A wedding processional is not necessary; neither are original wedding clothes, which may no longer become members of the wedding party. Instead, consider having younger family members or mannequins model the original fashions at the anniversary reception. Also, if the anniversary bride is not saving her wedding gown for a family heirloom, she may choose to use some of the lace or fabric in a new party dress for her anniversary celebration. Wedding bouquets and boutonnieres, identical to the originals, make sentimental accents. The original wedding gloves, jewelry, purse, or hankie are also perfect additions to a new anniversary ensemble.

Other wedding traditions are appropriate and sentimental reminders for the silver wedding. These include photos of the wedding party, a reception line, sharing wedding cake, and a silver goblet anniversary toast. Play the couple's "song" for a first dance introduction. Consider adding these other silver wedding traditions:

• Renew wedding vows and then dance under a silvery moon.

• Have each guest share a silver-lined memory of the anniversary couple.

• Take a group photo of the anniversary couple and their guests.

• Take instant photos of the anniversary couple and each guest as an anniversary party favor.

• Show a special video of short takes from the couple's home movie memories.

• Set up a *Newlywed Game* skit. Have a "game show host" ask the anniversary wife questions while the anniversary husband is taken out of the room. He will then be brought back to answer questions, trying to match his answers with his wife's. She is then asked to leave the room and the husband answers questions, and so on.

• Stage a *This Is Your Life* skit, reviewing memorable occasions and fun times the couple has enjoyed over the years.

• Hire a DJ, live band, or orchestra for dancing entertainment. Play the couple's favorite tunes including music from the year they were married.

• Present a fashion show featuring fashion changes over the couple's married years. If possible, use actual clothing from their early years including their original wedding costumes.

• For the anniversary couple: Take a special moment (separate from the anniversary party) to write silver-penned thank-you notes to all those who have helped your marriage be happy and successful.

Menu Ideas

Recreate the wedding menu (including the wedding cake, if possible). Or, have the chef prepare this silver-lined menu:

- Hors d'oeuvres served on a silver tray including silver demitasse spoons filled with salmon mousse and caviar
- Gleaming silver tureens of truffle soup
- Filet of swordfish topped with dill sauce and almonds
- Silver dollar potato pancakes
- Silver chafing dish of Brussels sprouts with glazed chestnuts
- Mini silver moon croissants tied with silver ribbons and served with butter and homemade jams
- Silver charm cake (Bake silver charm cake fortunes in the anniversary cake beforehand. Wrap silver charms in aluminum foil to make identification easy. Display the charm meanings in a silver frame set next to the cake. For example, a wishbone charm signifies luck and a heart signifies true love. The charms can also be attached to ribbons and placed under the edge of the cake for a charm pull.
- Silver-lining anniversary cake (Guests will feel like they're eating a fortune with a cake lined with edible, decorative accent sheets. See *Supplier Resource Directory* for source.)

Party Favors with Flair

Present guests with a silver wedding memento.

- Silver candied almonds wrapped in tulle bundles tied with silver rings and a silver ribbon
- Chocolate-dipped silver spoon sprinkled with silver candy decorations (Wrap the bowl of the spoon in cellophane and tie it with a silver ribbon. The silver potpourri spoon invitations described below in *A Silver Tea* also make nice party favors.)
- Silver vase with a single passion red rose
- Small silver frame with a photo of the wedding couple
- Small tulle-wrapped bundle of silver coins
- Silver "kiss-a-gram" bells mentioned in the *Decorating Touches* section
- Small gift-wrapped box containing a silver dollar

- Silver charm pull attached to a long silver ribbon, as described in the *Menu Ideas* section above (Charm pulls also make a decorative accent tied around a single-serving cake box. Tradition states that guests should place them under their pillows to dream of their true loves. See *Supplier Resource Directory* for source.)
- Silver-dipped or painted rose

A Silver Tea

The silver anniversary tea was known in our great-grandmothers' day as an informal, at-home celebration. Even Emily Post considered teas casual compared to formal receptions. "A tea" she said, "no matter how formal it pretends to be, is friendly and inviting." Today, the afternoon tea carries a more prim-and-proper image, but it's still an intimate and delightful affair.

Invite guests to this charming silver tea with a silver spoon invitation. Fill the bowl of a silver spoon with fragrant potpourri. Wrap the bowl with lace and tie it with a silk ribbon at the bottom of the spoon neck. Attach invitation details directly to the spoon.

Prepare for the silver tea by covering the table with a damask or lace tablecloth, setting it with a silver tea service at one end and a silver coffee service at the other end. If you prefer, a silver punch bowl filled with sparkling punch can replace the coffee service. Between the two services, place doily-lined silver platters of fancy finger sandwiches, tiny cream puffs, tulle-wrapped silver bells filled with nuts and candy mints, and petits fours. Place a round, double-layer wedding cake on a raised silver cake plate as the table centerpiece.

Silver Mine of Love

For twenty-five years, the couple has excavated the silver mine of love. Why not throw a western boomtown celebration full of silver and strike-it-rich fun? Send a silver dollar with this invitation message: "Dar's silver in dem dar hills!" Ask guests to dress with silver western flair, wearing silver spurs, silver belt buckles, and silver six-shooters (costume props). Illuminate a darkened room with lanterns, miners' hats, miners' hammers, picks, and shovels. Place an ore cart on tracks on one side of the room to collect anniversary gifts. Fill another ore cart with Coors Silver Bullet Beer.

Cover picnic tables with red-and-white-checked tablecloths. For centerpieces, place a mining lantern (a camping lantern painted silver) in the center of a mining pan overflowing with silver coins. Place a "dynamite" favor at each place setting. Wrap a cardboard bathroom tissue tube with silver paper. Place in it beforehand a piece of paper with a number written on it that corresponds to a door prize. Fasten a string or ribbon "fuse" to one end with one of these messages: "Twenty-five Years of Dynamite Love!" or "The Flame's Still Alive at Twenty-five!"

Share some "yippee-i-o" fun with an old-time western piano player or a player piano set up at the back of the room. The anniversary groom can win his gal's heart again by arranging for a preacher to ride in and reaffirm their marriage vows. Then it's time to go for the silver with some boomtown, strike-it-rich gaming tables including poker, roulette, and craps.

Silver Sword of Zorro

This bold Spanish-themed anniversary party is marked by the silver sword of Zorro. Invite guests by sending a black satin eye mask in a black box marked with a silver "Z." Ask guests to hide their identities behind these masks and to dress in all-black.

Lead guests along a path lined with flaming torches and strewn with flower petals. Carve a silver "Z" on the outside of the front door and greet guests with characters dressed as conquistadors and flamenco dancers. Guests will dine and dance among the intoxicating smell of pepper trees and the invigorating chords of the flamenco guitar.

Have a Zorro-clad figure lurk mysteriously among the crowd gathered in a Spanish villa courtyard. Surround the courtyard with stucco-like wall and arch facades wrapped with garlands of greenery and red flowers. Scatter preserved pepper tree leaves on the ground and on the tables. Light the area with iron-wall sconces and floor-stand torches. Cover tables with glass-domed, flower-filled silver vases and glass-enclosed silver candlesticks. Lay a single rose across each plate. Then drape the men's chairs with black Zorrolike capes and Spanish wide-brimmed hats. Place a lovely Spanish lace fan on each lady's seat along with a gift-wrapped Spanish hair comb.

Entertain guests throughout the evening with silver Spanish splendor. Dance to mood-provoking Spanish music, project a black and white Zorro movie or TV show tape against a stucco wall, and stage a Zorro silver sword match.

Anniversary Gift Suggestions

Here's a silver mine of anniversary gift ideas:

- Silver-plated music box
- Silver dinner bell
- Silver tray engraved with the anniversary date
- Silver candlesticks or candelabra
- Silver vase filled with twenty-five roses
- Silver photo frame or album
- Silver ice bucket
- Set of silver wine goblets
- Tickets for an overnight trip on a "silver streak" train
- Gift certificate for a "Hi-ho, Silver!" vacation at a western dude ranch
- Gift certificate for a silver bells sleigh ride
- Twenty-five silver dollars or a twenty-five dollar gift certificate
- Matching silver bracelets
- Personal jewelry, such as a silver charm bracelet or silver tie tack, exchanged between the couple
- Champagne-and-roses ride in a silver limousine
- Pair of airline tickets to the land of the "silver screen" (Hollywood)

A Special Moment for the Anniversary Couple

From sunrise to sunset, choose from a variety of just-for-two silver anniversary adventures.

Breakfast in Bed

Treat your spouse to breakfast in bed served on a silver tray with a rose-filled silver vase and the morning's newspaper. Anne Morrow Lindbergh once said, "A simple enough pleasure, surely, to have breakfast alone with one's husband, but how seldom married people in the midst of life achieve it."

Silver Bullet Fun

Keep the home fires burning by cuddling up and watching silver bullet movies. Choose Lone Ranger or other silver bullet films or hide in each other's arms for frightening silver bullet werewolf stories.

A Silver Countryside Picnic

Take off for a little silver adventure of your own. Arrange for a silver limousine to take you to the countryside for a picnic lunch.

Silver Streak Mystery

Blindfold your spouse for a mystery trip. Take him or her to the train station for a "silver streak" train ride.

Moonlight Hayride

Take your spouse for a moonlight hayride or sleigh ride on the evening of your twenty-fifth anniversary.

A Walk under the Silvery Moon

Go for a romantic walk, holding hands under the silvery moon.

The Thirtieth Anniversary
—Pearl—

Toast: Here's to a marriage sailing on a sea of pearls!
May your joys be as deep as the ocean and your
misfortunes as light as the foam.
—Inspired by a Freixenet toast

The pearl has traditionally been the symbol of the thirtieth wedding anniversary. There are many legends associated with pearls —the jewel of the sea. Ancient Chinese legend claims pearls were conceived in the brains of dragons. The dragons would then guard the symbols of wisdom between their teeth. Only the brave would attempt to slay the dragons to claim their precious treasures. Hindu stories propose that pearls evolved from clouds, elephants, and wild boars. The Greeks and Persians believed pearls came from oysters touched by drops of rain or dew. Those in the Orient believed pearls were the tears of angels, mermaids, and mythical nymphs. These traditional tales nicely complement the legendary love of a thirty-year marriage.

Sailing on a Sea of Pearls

One legend tells of pearls born from moonbeams shining upon the ocean. Like the legend, this sea-of-pearls celebration is filled with the mysteries of the sea.

Invitation Ideas

Send guests a one-of-a-kind pearl anniversary party invitation.

- String of pearls (Buy an inexpensive dime-store string.)
- Clamshell decorated with pearl beads
- Invitation placed in a pearl-decorated frame
- Toy sailboat filled with pearls (Glue pearls inside or on top of the boat.)
- Sailor's or captain's hat decorated with pearl beads
- Pearl-trimmed, engraved invitation

Special Instructions for Guests

Please compose a "pearl of wisdom" to share with the anniversary couple.

Decorating Touches

Hold this sea-of-love celebration on a yacht, at a seaside or lakeside restaurant, or in a nautical restaurant. You can also create a pearl fantasy.

- Cover tables with iridescent pearl tablecloths. Raise a ship's sail on each guest table. Attach a sail to a pole placed through the hole of an umbrella table and secured with the umbrella base. Fashion the sail from a white bed sheet or piece of cloth. Place the bottom of the sail high enough to allow guests to view each other from across the table.
- Encircle the pole of the ship's sail with life-preserver centerpieces. Place a bottle of champagne in the center of a small life-preserver decoration. Inscribe each life preserver with nautical notations such as "S. S. Love Boat" or "Sea of Love."

- For another centerpiece idea, wrap pearls around the base of a boat model or sailor figure.
- Place a royal blue napkin tied with a string of pearls at each place setting.
- Hang a sailor's or captain's hat on the back of each chair.
- Write the name of each guest on a plastic toy boat trimmed with pearl beads.
- Accent the table décor with pearl-trimmed votive candle holders and pearl-framed menu card holders.
- Hang colorful triangle flags, intertwined with pearl garland, from the ceiling.
- Cover the dance floor with white pearlized balloons.
- Set up an actual sailboat in the room as a food buffet or drink bar.

Theme-Inspired Activities and Entertainment

Sail on a sea of pearls celebration.

- Guide guests to their tables with this "just ducky" table assignment activity: Float rubber ducks covered in pearl beads in a child's pool. Invite each couple to choose a duck. Print table numbers on the bottoms of the ducks beforehand.
- Offer a "bubbly" toast to the bride and groom: Blow bubbles at the couple after sharing an anniversary toast.
- Read aloud the "pearls of wisdom" notes brought by guests.
- Provide dance music for the guests' pleasure on the ship's bridge. Ask the DJ to play "Sea of Love" and other nautical favorites.
- Gather guests together to make paper boats and to conduct a regatta.
- Send the anniversary couple on a pearl odyssey for their anniversary gifts. String pearl garlands through party rooms leading to a hidden gift table.
- Hire an interactive entertainment company to set up a remote control boats activity.
- Hire a storyteller to narrate some legendary high seas adventures and mythical stories.

- Christen this love-boat celebration by breaking a bottle of champagne over a ship prop or against the outside of the building (obtain permission from the site, of course). The celebration can also be christened by popping the cork over a champagne-glass-filled boat prop or a pyramid of champagne glasses.

Menu Ideas

Cover the sailboat with a specially cut wooden cover and load it up with a sumptuous seafood buffet. Provide additional nautical-clad wait staff to serve elderly or physically challenged guests.

- Include lobster, crab, shrimp, a variety of fish, clams, and other seafood dishes.
- Set up a separate oyster and pearl bar swirled with strings of pearls.
- Set up beef and turkey carving stations.
- Decorate a cheese and fruit buffet around clam-shaped ice sculptures.
- Serve guests a tossed salad in toy-boat salad bowls before inviting them to visit the buffets.
- Serve vodka gimlets with pearl onion garnishes.
- Have a specialty cake designed as a 3-D sailing ship floating on a sea of pearls.

Party Favors with Flair

Present each guest with an oyster treasure as a memento of this sea-of-love celebration.

- For the ladies, an inexpensive pearl pendant necklace in a clam or oyster shell wrapped in tulle and a nautical blue ribbon
- For the men, an inexpensive pearl tie tack in the shell described above
- Toy boats filled with candy and decorated with pearl beads
- The pearl-decorated sailor's or captain's hats placed on each chair
- Individual, miniature bottles of champagne tied with pearl strand bows
- Pearl-decorated wedding-bubble bottles

A Pearl-Filled Odyssey

Citizens of ancient Rome wore pearls as a symbol of purity and sumptuousness. Romans also believed pearls would bring marital happiness, so grooms frequently gave pearls to their brides on their wedding day. Adapt this tradition to a pearl-filled odyssey designed to ensure a splendid anniversary party. Invite guests with a scroll invitation from Juno, the Roman goddess of marriage. Roll and seal the scroll with a wax insignia and tie it with a string of pearls. Then issue a "When in Rome, do as the Romans" declaration asking guests to wear togas to the party.

Create a Romanesque atmosphere. Hang a print of Botticelli's *The Birth of Venus*, which depicts the Roman goddess of love and beauty rising from her birthplace—the foam of the sea. Fill a water fountain or reflecting pool with pearls. Position stone-column fern holders and Romanesque urns throughout the room. Add a bust of Caesar and a stone sculpture garden and birdbath. Drape the room with ivy and cast romantic torch lighting upon the area. In the center of the room, place a pair of doves in a gilded cage draped with strings of pearl. Cover tables and chairs with pearl-colored cloths gathered with gold cording. Use Roman classical design chair covers (see the *Supplier Resource Directory* for source). For centerpieces, drape Romanesque statuettes such as Priapus, the Roman god of the gardens, with strings of pearls. Place these small sculptures on a tray covered with grapes, ivy, and lighted votive candles. Set each place setting with a clamshell laden with pearl bath beads as the place card. For a fun touch, write the names of each guest on a bottle of Caesar salad dressing wrapped with a bow made from a string of pearls.

In the ancient Roman custom, dramatically announce dinner. Have attendants blow through a conch shell and shower guests with rose petals dropped from the ceiling or a balcony. Next, have a toga-clad wait staff parade platters of elaborately placed food throughout the room. Cover large platters with Roman delicacies like roasted stuffed pig, celery and leeks in honey sauce served in pumpkin shells, and flaming yams (doused in brandy and ignited). Don't forget the Caesar salad! Decorate the anniversary cake with gold laurel leaf trim and pearl bead icing. Display Roman wedding cakes (honey fruitcakes) next to the cake. Give the anniversary couple a "coup de marriage" cup (a two-handled goblet) for a special anniversary toast. After dinner, bury an anniversary time capsule in the back yard or attic to be opened on a future anniversary. Fill time capsules with anniversary and marriage mementos.

Anniversary Gift Suggestions

Choose one of these pearl fantasy gifts:

- Pearl-trimmed or mother-of-pearl photo frame
- Pearl necklace, pearl tie tack, or pearl cuff links, exchanged between the anniversary couple
- Gift certificate for a local seafood restaurant
- Gift certificate for a dinner boat cruise
- Hawaiian cruise, purchased as a group gift by family and friends
- Champagne and pearl gift basket
- Photo album adorned with a rhinestone diamond heart or a copy of the movie *Diamonds Are Forever* (Diamonds are the modern gift designation for the thirtieth anniversary. More diamond gift ideas can be found in "The Sixtieth and Beyond Anniversary: Diamond" chapter.)

A Special Moment for the Anniversary Couple

A "Pearl Treasure" Card Shower

Have family and friends surprise the couple with this singular gift idea. Ask each member to send the couple an anniversary greeting card containing a single pearl bead. The couple will then collect the beads in a crystal bowl for a lasting pearl treasure from their family and friends. Also, present the couple with a pearl-decorated basket filled with a bottle of champagne, pearlescent champagne glasses, French bread, and a jar of caviar to savor as they treasure their anniversary greetings.

The Thirty-Fifth Anniversary
—Coral—

Toast: To love as intricate and beautiful as the coral bottom of the sea!

Thirty-five years of marriage nurtures a love as intricate and beautiful as the ocean's coral floor. For the perfect coral-themed anniversary party, imagine the adventure of an under-the-sea casino. Or, envision the charm of coralbell flowers and an old-fashioned ice cream social.

Coral Casino under the Sea

Take a dive into this coral fantasy. Deep beneath the sea in a coral cavern lies a casino nestled in seaweed, old ruins, and sunken chests. King Neptune presides over this under-the-sea coral casino grotto.

Invitation Ideas

Invite guests with one of these underwater accents:

- Box containing a beautiful piece of coral
- Fishnet bag of seashells and coral pieces

- Coral-colored plastic fish
- Poker chips and some small seashells in a fishnet bag
- Poker hand tied together with a ribbon threaded through a hole punched in a corner of each card (Choose a deck of sea-design playing cards.)

Special Instructions for Guests

See what you've caught! Bring the enclosed fish (actually a fish shape cut from coral-colored tissue paper inscribed with a prize number) to the underwater casino to claim your prize.

Decorating Touches

Lead guests through a bubble tunnel made with clear balloons to this underwater coral casino deep beneath the waves.

- Place a seaweed-looking arch at the party's entrance and play ocean wave music.
- Hang "swimming" fish and sea horses along with dangling "seaweed" from the ceiling for this underwater picture.
- Cover walls with shimmering seafoam green material. Line it with coral, starfish, sea horses, and seashells. Up-light the walls with spotlights placed on the floor pointing upward for a dramatic underwater shadow effect.
- Scatter fishnet, treasure chests, and sunken ship props about the room.
- Cover tables with shimmering coral-colored floor-length cloths and add shimmering green shell-shaped chair covers (See *Supplier Resource Directory* for source). Another idea for coral table covers involves layering pieces of coral, shells, starfish, and plastic fish between a coral-colored tablecloth and a layer of fishnet.
- Choose one of these underwater centerpieces:
  —Secure coral pieces with florist's clay to the bottom of clear globe-shaped bowls. Add a live goldfish and float a water lily in each bowl. The coral also looks spectacular next to a large, white underwater flower secured to the bottom of the bowl. Encircle the centerpiece with tea lights placed on lily pads. After the party, give away the goldfish bowls as door prizes. Or, you might be able to work

out a special arrangement with your local pet store. Suggest renting the bowls and goldfish for both a small fee and an advertising gesture like placing the pet store's business card near the bowl.

—Place a hurricane lamp over a pillar candle. Inside the hurricane glass, surround the outside of the candle with seashells and coral.

—Space a trio of taper candles in a low crystal bowl with florist's clay. Fill the bottom of the bowl with sand and add seashells and coral.

- Use seashells with tiny spoons for salt and pepper containers.
- Attach a place card, printed with the guest's name, to a piece of coral.
- Situate a live mermaid-character centerpiece on the food buffet or bar or in a room vignette. She can recline on a rock and talk to passersby, or you can have her lie completely still throughout the party.
- Cover the dance floor "sea bottom" with coral-colored balloons.
- Set up the party next to a pool.

Theme-Inspired Activities and Entertainment

Welcome guests to King Neptune's under-the-sea coral casino grotto with this underwater fun:

- Set up professional, Las Vegas-style casino games including blackjack tables, roulette wheels, craps tables, and slot machines.
- Provide a big band sound for dancing in the coral garden.
- Hire a mermaid harpist. (If you can't get the real thing, ask an entertainment agency to arrange for a harpist to dress in a mermaid costume.)
- Exchange "tissue" fish enclosed with invitations for door prizes.
- If holding this under-the-sea gala near a pool, treat guests to a water ballet performance. You could also conduct an underwater treasure hunt for the lost coral treasure.

Menu Ideas

Hold an old-fashioned fish fry and serve these "What a catch!" mouthwatering delights:

- Fried codfish and perch
- Baked salmon
- Hush puppies and French fries
- Green peas and pearl onions
- Seaweed (fresh coleslaw)
- Shrimp cocktails
- Octopus punch (Use rubber snakes to simulate outstretched octopus legs from the punch bowl.)
- Decorate a round- or sheet-cake-shaped anniversary cake with white icing. Write "Happy Coral Anniversary" with blue cake-decorating gel. Then decorate the sides of the cake with a frosting made of removable seashell and coral trim. Place the anniversary cake on a cake board, secured to a life preserver floating in an inflated plastic child's pool. Add goldfish to the water.

Party Favors with Flair

Guests will want to dry off after leaving this underwater adventure. Give each guest a coral-colored bath or beach towel. Here are some more underwater coral delights:

- Make Christmas tree ornaments from coral pieces.
- Make and give coral pendant necklaces and coral tie tacks.
- Give each guest a ribbon-tied plastic food bag containing a goldfish.
- Wrap coral-colored, shell-shaped guest soaps in a ribbon-tied cellophane bag.
- Wrap Gummi fish in a clear gift bag. Tie with a wide coral-satin bow.
- Give ocean-sound relaxation cassettes or CDs as party favors.
- Give out decks of "Go Fish" playing cards.
- Decorate clear, vinyl pool tote bags with plastic fish, coral, and netting.

Coralbells and an Old-Fashioned Ice Cream Social

Step back in time with an old-fashioned ice cream social. Send guests an ice cream cone glued to an "ice cream dip" of a small coral-colored balloon. Write invitation details directly on the balloon or enclose a note with the ice cream cone concoction. Hold this festive anniversary celebration in the park or create an indoor parklike atmosphere. Set out park benches under potted trees. Decorate with coralbell flowers and hang "coralbells" (coral-colored tissue bells) from the top of a white-lattice gazebo or trellis. Cover the ground with coral-colored tablecloth blankets secured on each corner with a rock. Set each "table" with a basket filled with coralbell-planted clay pots.

Have turn-of-the-century (nineteenth century) costumed-characters, complete with bowler hats and parasols, stroll through the crowd. From the white-latticed gazebo, have an old-fashioned barbershop quartet entertain guests. The quartet should be dressed in red-and-white-striped vests and skimmers (straw, flat-topped, wide-brimmed hats). Perhaps a "coral bells" performance (coral-painted bells ringing) could also be arranged by recruiting the younger kids in the family. Then hand out coral-painted pinwheels and small coral-satin-ribbon-tied lace bags filled with coral-colored taffy. Don't forget the ice cream social fun. Make homemade ice cream and root beer floats. Feed ducks in the pond, play croquet, ride tandem bikes, and hold a "build-the-tallest-ice-cream-cone" contest.

Anniversary Gift Suggestions

The mermaid siren calls for one of these romantic, underwater-themed gifts:

- Oil painting of the sea
- Sea blue bowl filled with coral pieces
- Gift certificate for a seaside cottage weekend or indoor poolside fun at a local hotel (Pack the certificate in a picnic basket filled with bathing suits, beach towels, and inflatable beach balls.)
- Gift certificate to a seafood restaurant
- Matching fishing vests and tackle boxes filled with fishing lore

- Aquarium filled with freshwater fish
- Coral jewelry
- Set of jade bookends, jade jewelry, or jade knickknacks (Jade is the modern thirty-fifth anniversary gift suggestion.)

A Special Moment for the Anniversary Couple

A Walk by the Sea

Take a walk by the seaside or lakeside, just the two of you. If weather or location circumstances don't permit, treat yourselves to a sea salt foot soak. Fill a child's inflatable pool with water and moisturizing sea salts and place it at the edge of your living room couch. Put on an ocean-wave relaxation tape and dip your bare feet in this "sea water." Then close your eyes, hold hands, and visualize the seashore.

The Fortieth Anniversary
—Ruby—

Toast: Together, your hearts sparkle like precious rubies;
Your marriage is a treasured gem!

The ruby is considered one of the most precious gemstones. Thus it is an appropriate symbol for the fortieth wedding anniversary. In China and India, the ruby is worn to promote happiness and health. What better way to celebrate the inestimable happiness and health of the fortieth anniversary couple's marriage than with this priceless jewel!

Take a Magic Carpet Ride!

Invite guests to take a magic carpet ride to this "sheik" affair where ruby-colored Persian carpets abound and ruby-adorned genies grant wishes. Veiled with Middle Eastern mystique, anniversary guests are sure to delight in this priceless night of magic.

Invitation Ideas

"His royal highness, the Sultan of Love, hereby requests your presence at the Feast of the Jeweled Anniversary in his ruby palace." Send this royal decree along with one of these invitation jewels:

- Scroll rolled and tied with a ruby red cord (Drop the scroll and faux ruby rhinestones into a corked glass or plastic bottle. See *Supplier Resource Directory* for source.)
- Plastic or inflatable magic lamp in a gift box filled with faux ruby gems.
- Invitation details written on a piece of "magic" carpet
- Ostrich fan decorated with faux ruby rhinestones
- The invitation placed in a trinket or jewelry box decorated with rubylike jewels
- Engraved invitation trimmed with ruby rhinestones
- Invitation details printed on a post card or note card depicting an *Aladdin* or *I Dream of Jeannie* scene

Special Instructions for Guests

Bring three wishes to grant the anniversary couple.

Decorating Touches

Transform the party area into a land of Middle Eastern mystique.
- Park a ruby red "flying" carpet in front of the ruby palace.
- Place a sign in front of the party area that reads, "Camel Parking Behind Palace."
- Tent the ceiling and walls with sheer ruby red gossamer cloth.
- Arrange a gold-painted, keyhole-shaped doorway for the palace entrance. Add a curtain of ruby red beads. Have a sultanlike character pull the ruby curtain back as each guest passes through.
- Hang a flying carpet from the ceiling. Use a Persian-design rug or some ruby-colored material.
- Add gold urns of palm trees around the room, with rubies scattered at their bases.
- Cast a wish over the "rubies" sprinkled on the bottom of a reflective pool or water fountain. Float ruby red rose blooms or petals on the water's surface.
- Hang brass lanterns above the tables for romantic ambiance.
- Add a peacock prop decorated with faux ruby gems.

- Fill the tented room with large, tufted, gold- and ruby-colored floor pillows.
- Project Rudolph Valentino's black-and-white silent movie *The Sheik* or an *Aladdin* movie on a white curtain wall.
- Cover tables in ruby splendor:
  - Place several tables together to make one long table. Cover it with ruby-colored cloth and add gold lamé chair covers. (See *Supplier Resource Directory* for source.) Wrap ruby-studded sashes around the lower chair backs.
  - Glue ruby baubles on pewter or silver goblets. (Try your local thrift store or flea market for inexpensive pewter, silver, and brassware.)
  - Use ruby red glassware and plateware accented with brass saucers and chargers.
  - Wrap gold lamé napkins with ruby-studded napkin rings. Glue ruby baubles onto brass or other napkin rings.
  - Sew ruby beads to the edges of each napkin.
  - Make a royal place card by attaching a ruby-colored tassel to a white, oversized place card inscribed with ruby or gold ink.
- Set each table with one of these ruby centerpiece jewels:
  - A gold-colored pewter or silver vase covered with faux ruby gems (Fill with ruby roses or dramatic peacock feathers.)
  - Brass containers filled with ruby red roses
  - Scattered piles of gold-painted fruit laid on raised brass cake stands and accented with faux ruby jewels
  - Sultan hats placed on hat stands (Glue a faux ruby on the front of the hat.)
  - *I Dream of Jeannie* bottles laden with faux rubies
  - Glass candlesticks and wineglasses wrapped with faux ruby jewels (String jewels on a wire and then wrap the wire around the glassware.)
  - Magic lamps adorned with ruby jewels
  - A fruit display stretching down the entire center of the table including plenty of grapes and pineapples (Write each guest's name with a gold paint pen on an additional piece of fruit, such as papaya, apple, or pear, and place it in front of his or her place setting.)

Theme-Inspired Activities and Entertainment

Take guests on a magic carpet ride of fun.

- Provide camel rides or camel photo opportunities.
- Provide Middle Eastern music and a belly dance revue.
- Stage a magic show or have a magician stroll through the crowd doing magic tricks. Arrange for the entertainer to dress in a Middle Eastern costume.
- Hire a snake charmer or sword swallower to entertain guests.
- Parade anniversary gifts on a magic carpet. Ceremoniously read a few of the wishes granted to the anniversary couple. Present the rest of the wishes on a brass, ruby-adorned platter for the couple to review at their leisure.
- Provide sheer ruby and gold lamé cloth to make turbans and veils for guests in a special Middle Eastern millinery shop.

Menu Ideas

Since this is a very sheik affair, have sheik-clad wait staff serve guests a Middle Eastern feast:

- Ruby red caviar served on toast triangles
- Date and orange spinach salad
- Jewel salads (Cut Jell-O into diamond shapes or use individual jewel-like molds.)
- Roasted chicken breast with artichokes
- Beef kabobs with currant pecan sauce
- Couscous
- Platter of figs, olives, pears, and dates
- Pita bread
- Ruby red wine poured from brass pitchers
- Flaming ruby red cherries jubilee dessert presented by belly dancers
- Anniversary cake, layered with ruby red raspberry, strawberry, or cherry filling and topped with ruby baubles (Surround the cake with plates of baklava. Parade the entire anniversary cake creation on a

magic carpet carried by the sheik's harem. Tip: Support the carpet with a firm tray or board.)

- Bowl of ruby red punch

Party Favors with Flair

Send each guest home with a jewel to remember this ruby red anniversary celebration.

- Ruby red pistachios wrapped in clear cellophane wrap and decorated with ruby baubles or wrapped in a ruby-colored scarf
- Ruby-bauble-adorned trinket boxes
- Small bottles of perfume and men's cologne decorated with faux ruby jewels
- Single ruby red rose
- Ruby costume jewelry such as a brooch, pendant, or tie tack

Ruby Tea Dance

A nostalgic tea dance is a touching way to celebrate this precious anniversary. The charming Victorian tea dance became popular at the Waldorf Astoria Hotel at the end of World War I. Hold this grand event in a grand ballroom. Encircle the dance floor with tables covered with white cloths and showered with ruby rhinestones. To each table, add ruby red glass votives or a small table lamp with a ruby-trimmed lampshade.

Ease into the afternoon with a sparkling glass of ruby red champagne made by adding drops of red food coloring to a chilled bottle of champagne. Savor a traditional afternoon tea, starting with a quartet of tea sandwiches: ribbon, cucumber, salmon, and curried chicken cream puffs. Accompany this with warm cranberry scones and Devonshire clotted cream. Serve pots of steaming hot tea including Earl Grey, Darjeeling, or Ruby Red (cranberry). Top off this culinary afternoon tea with the grand finale—ruby jewel desserts. From a tiered serving tray, offer these ruby red treats: strawberry jam heart-shaped tarts, white-glazed petits fours graced with a single ruby rhinestone (made with gel icing), ruby red strawberries dipped in white chocolate, and white anniversary cake made with a ruby red raspberry filling.

Then waltz or foxtrot the afternoon away on a ruby red glittered floor (use Mylar confetti) to the romantic music of a small orchestra hired especially for the occasion. Or, sit back and listen to beautiful Mozart pieces, Viennese waltzes, big band hits, or passionate tangos. Send guests home with a china teacup and saucer candle. Fill teacups with ruby red wax and a candlewick. Sprinkle the top with crystal glitter.

Anniversary Gift Suggestions

Present a ruby gift to the couple:

- Basket of ruby red apples or ruby grapefruit
- Ruby red glassware such as a vase, wineglasses, or candlesticks
- Ruby necklace and ruby tie tack or cuff links
- Ruby-decorated photo frame
- Persian rug
- Palm plant
- Garden-side water fountain or reflecting pool filled with ruby baubles
- Forty ruby red roses
- Forty dollar gift certificate or check placed in an envelope with ruby rhinestones
- Matching ruby rings

A Special Moment for the Anniversary Couple

A Ruby Red Kiss

Prepare a night of romance for the anniversary couple with an intimate candlelight dinner for two. Cover the table in crisp white linen and ruby red candlesticks. Shower ruby lover's kisses (ruby rhinestones) over the precious-jewel table settings. Trim white linen napkins with the same. Set the table with red glassware. After dinner, sneak away to the kitchen and clean up. (Don't let the couple help, no matter what they say.) Then leave the anniversary couple alone to share a private ruby red anniversary kiss.

The Forty-Fifth Anniversary
—Sapphire—

Toast: To a marriage the color of sapphire—
Its color: pure love, wisdom, and devotion!

Precious as the sapphire stone, a forty-five year marriage is a treasure that should be displayed for all to admire. The celebration ideas that follow allow the anniversary couple to reflect on the moments that true-blue love carried them through.

Titanic Jewel of Love

Take a luxury cruise on a sapphire sea of love with a Titanic anniversary adventure. Fortunately, this ship is unsinkable. Borrow some of the immense glamour and romance of the legendary cruise liner as well as the mystery of the sapphire-colored heart necklace.

Invitation Ideas

Invite "passenger" guests with a first-class luxury-liner ticket. Send an engraved invitation with one of these Titanic ideas:

- Life preserver prop inscribed with the word "Titanic"
- Replica of the necklace worn in the 1998 movie *Titanic* (See the *Supplier Resource Directory* for a commercial source or make one by covering a wooden heart with blue glitter, adding silver glitter trim, and attaching the piece to a thin silver ribbon.)
- Small model, key chain, or charm of the *Titanic*, placed in a gift box with small sapphirelike jewels
- Sailor's hat inscribed with the word "R.M.S. Titanic"
- Reproduction of a telegraph message, providing party details
- Invitation cut into a *Titanic* shape with printed detail in sapphire-blue ink
- Luggage tag trimmed with a sapphire rhinestone.

Special Instructions for Guests

Join us in a special bon voyage toast to the unsinkable love of Michael and Ann. Please bring a sapphire-colored wineglass to present to the anniversary couple for a memorable and titanic collection.

Decorating Touches

Re-create the first-class opulence of the White Star Line's ill-fated luxury liner, the R.M.S. *Titanic*.

- Greet guests at the party entrance with a rope-handled loading ramp and ship's deck. Have a ship's crew member collect passage tickets while standing next to a *Titanic* poster or a poster depicting cruise passengers loading a luxury liner. Display the poster on a velvet-backed and gilded-framed marquis. Build a more elaborate entrance with wall murals or decorator-built facades. Add portholes, life preservers, a vintage traveling trunk, and a stack of luggage topped with a vintage birdcage.
- Play the soundtrack from the 1998 movie *Titanic* as guests enter the first-class dining area.
- Serve dinner to guests in an elaborately decorated private room of an elegant restaurant. Or, create a Titanic stage:

—Line a black-draped wall with a gigantic silhouette of the *Titanic,* using twinkle lights.

—Line a wall with portholes backed with sapphire blue paper for guests to look out upon the ocean. Or, fill the portholelike frames with photo scenes from the anniversary couple's life.

—Decorate the back of an orchestra stage with a backdrop painting of a luxury liner's hull. Trim the orchestra seating with deck railing to simulate the bow of a ship. Add a smokestack prop with special-effect smoke and horn sounds.

• Cover tables with fine white linen and choose one of these *Titanic*-inspired centerpieces:

—A model of the *Titanic* with a replica of the famous necklace draped over it

—Elaborate floral arrangements with vintage-looking table lamps

—Silver candelabra with green vine and sapphirelike stone accents at its base

• Set the table with fine china and crystal. If possible, use a china pattern similar to that actually used in first class on the famed luxury ship (a royal blue design trimmed in gold). As pictured in many *Titanic* photos, fold linen napkins in bishop's miter folds. This common fold can be found in any napkin-folding book.

• Decorate the room with *Titanic* memorabilia including a half-finished *Titanic* jigsaw puzzle left on a side table next to a chair, framed *Titanic* and luxury liner posters, a *Titanic*-design blanket thrown over a side chair, and so on.

Theme-Inspired Activities and Entertainment

Set sail with these fun Titanic activities.

• Pass out vintage turn-of-the-century hats, furs, long gloves, evening bags, feather boas, dinner coats, and an abundance of faux sapphire jewelry to guests as they come in the door. Rent enough costume accessories for all the guests beforehand from a costume rental store. Have a photographer take instant photos of guests during dinner and present them later with an "I survived the Titanic" photo frame.

- Take instant photo favors in a lifeboat prop painted with the phrase "Unsinkable Love."
- Hire an Unsinkable Molly Brown character to provide walk-around entertainment.
- Have a string quartet entertain guests as the ship "goes down."
- Present the anniversary couple with a memento from each guest: a mixed and matched sapphire blue glass collection. Pack it in a vintage suitcase.

Menu Ideas

Enjoy a decadent nine-course meal inspired by the actual menu served to first-class passengers on that fateful April 14, 1912. Since the exact preparation and ingredients are unknown (their secrets and recipes having gone down with the ship), have your chef create his or her interpretation of this glorious feast. You may want to reduce the number of courses and selections to suit today's tastes. Include a dessert course of wedding anniversary cake with a special anniversary toast. (See the following page for a first-class dinner from an actual *Titanic* menu.)

A different wine was served with each course. Fresh fruit and cheeses were available following the last course. After your anniversary dinner, invite guests to a drawing room for coffee, port, and distilled spirits. No need to separate the ladies and the men as was the custom. However, you may want to provide a separate area for cigar smokers. Provide cigar favors for this activity.

Party Favors with Flair

As you bid these Titanic passengers farewell, send them off with one of these sapphire jewels.
- Piece of costume jewelry with a sapphire heart design
- *Titanic* model
- *Titanic* key chain, charm, or other ship replica

R.M.S. TITANIC

April 14, 1912

Hors d'Oeuvre Variés
Oysters

Consommé Olga   Cream of Barley

Salmon, Mousseline Sauce, Cucumber

Filet Mignon Lili
Sauté of Chicken Lyonnaise
Vegetable Marrow Farçie

Lamb, Mint Sauce
Roast Duckling, Apple Sauce
Sirloin of Beef   Chateau Potatoes

Green Peas   Creamed Carrots
Boiled Rice
Parmentier & Boiled New Potatoes

Punch Romaine

Roast Squab & Cress
Cold Asparagus Vinaigrette
Pâté de Foie Gras
Celery

Waldorf Pudding
Peaches in Chartreuse Jelly
Chocolate & Vanilla Eclairs

French Ice Cream

- Brandy snifter filled with sapphirelike jewels
- Chocolate *Titanic* ship mold with a rock-candy iceberg (Check a chocolate candy specialty store or see the *Supplier Resource Directory* for sources.)
- Piece of *Titanic* reproduction memorabilia
- Copy of the 1998 movie *Titanic* or an earlier version of the story
- Cassette tape or CD of the soundtrack from the 1998 movie *Titanic*
- Bottle of champagne tied with a sapphire bow
- Personally inscribed banded cigar

Rhapsody in Blue

Color this anniversary party rhapsody-in-blue. Send invitations to the couple's blue-book guest list. Tie an invitation trimmed with sapphire blue rhinestones to a brilliant blue helium balloon. Place both inside a sapphire blue, gift-wrapped box, keeping the sharp rhinestones separated from the balloon. Once opened, the balloon will float up with a special anniversary party message. Ask guests to dress in sapphire blue in honor of the anniversary couple.

Decorate the entire party area in blue. (Hint: Add lighting and neutral white accents to help increase depth perception for practical maneuverability.) Drape an entry arch with sheer white chiffon sparkling with sapphirelike gemstones. Hang a white or silver cage of bluebirds of happiness on each side of the entryway. Up-light the party room walls with blue and white lighting. Add fountains of water highlighted with a sapphire blue tone.

Lay shimmering sapphire blue tablecloths over floor-length, white satin cloths. Add matching sapphire blue chair covers. Top this blue elegance with transparent cobalt blue vases filled with battery-operated twinkle lights. Extend white ostrich feathers, dusted with a hint of blue glitter, from the vases. Place these brilliant centerpieces on mirror tiles and sweep the bases with clouds of sheer white tulle and small glass votive candles to send romantic reflections across the table. Sprinkle blue Mylar confetti over the tulle and mirror base. Wrap rolled white linen napkins with dangling sapphire-rhinestone strings and lay one on a white china plate at each place setting.

Serve a rhapsody-in-blue dinner by having guests rotate to a new, predetermined seat for each course. Carefully calculate the moves in advance. The cue to moving to a new table is the playing of *Rhapsody in Blue* and a friendly reminder by the MC. The menu includes the following: fresh romaine lettuce topped with julienne vegetables and served with bleu cheese dressing, chicken cordon bleu, clouds of mashed potatoes served on a sky blue lining, blue-ribbon vegetable melody, warm blueberry muffins with whipped butter, and a blue pièce d'occasion—individual blueberry cheesecakes decorated as miniature wedding cakes.

Cover the dance floor with white opalescent and sapphire blue balloons. Hang a mirror ball above the room to cast sparkling romance over the dance floor. Dance to *Rhapsody in Blue* and Broadway show tunes.

Anniversary Gift Suggestions

Select one of these gifts full of true-blue romance and titanic adventure.

- Dinner certificate to a seafood restaurant or a dinner-boat cruise
- Titanic gift basket filled with a luxury cruise liner coffee table book, champagne, sapphire blue champagne glasses, a soundtrack of the 1998 movie *Titanic*, and a collection of *Titanic* movies
- Remember Jack's artistic talent in the 1998 movie? Commission an artist to create a drawing or an oil painting of the anniversary couple—in more modest attire, of course.
- Matching sapphire rings or sapphire jewelry (maybe a *Titanic* necklace replica)
- Cruise aboard a luxury liner
- Cruise or ticket to Alaska to view the sapphire blue beauty and magnificent colors of the northern lights—the aurora borealis.

A Special Moment for the Anniversary Couple

A Sapphire Rainbow

The next time you're together and you see a rainbow—stop. Look for the sapphire blue band and reflect on your happy years together and the love you share. If you can't wait for an outdoor rainbow, try hiding a crystal pendant hung on a silver ribbon in a sapphire blue velvet jewelry gift box. Present it to your spouse and hang it from the window in front of the sun's rays. Then gaze upon the rainbow and remember the wonderful moments you've shared.

Sapphire Sky Message

Your love will soar into the wild blue yonder with this idea. Hire an airplane company or advertising agency to write your "Happy Anniversary" love message with smoke in the sapphire blue sky.

The Fiftieth Anniversary
—Gold—

Toast: "She is mine own, and I as rich in having
such a jewel as twenty seas,
if all their sands were pearl,
the water nectar and the rocks pure gold."

—William Shakespeare

All golden anniversary celebrations are tributes to resilient, loving fifty-year marriages. For those fortunate enough to have been blessed with a lifelong love, the fiftieth anniversary is an event of a lifetime. Celebrate this anniversary with a grand "Golden Fiftieth Anniversary Gala." Or, create a more casual yet magical affair such as a "Fifties Sock Hop," a "Ropin' Fifty Anniversary," or a "Swashbuckling Pirate's Gold Treasure."

Golden Fiftieth Anniversary Gala

Golden wedding bands symbolize eternal love. When devotion lasts fifty years, the marriage should be treasured like precious gold. Capture this golden moment with an unforgettable golden fiftieth anniversary gala or a golden-moments, at-home family dinner.

Invitation Ideas

Reunite the anniversary couple with family and friends and share golden memories of many happy years together.

- Choose an invitation with a gold, sentimental design. Print details with gold metallic ink. Place it in a gold, foil-lined envelope and add a gold foil seal as an exquisite touch.
- Place the invitation inside a gold top hat filled with gold Mylar gift shreds.
- Send a gold-lamé bow tie for each guest with a note reading, "Gold tie requested."
- Spray a 45 RPM record with gold paint for a "gold record" invitation.
- Have an invitation hand-delivered by a white-gloved delivery person wearing a tuxedo and holding a bouquet of gold Mylar, helium-filled balloons.
- Enclose a single gold-painted rose with the invitation.
- Enclose a gilded leaf with the invitation.
- Send a sequined and feathered gold mask or gold-painted *Phantom of the Opera* mask with the invitation.
- Let Cupid's love arrow fly by sending a gold-painted cupid's-toy bow and arrow.
- Send an invitation displayed in a gold photo frame.
- Print the invitation details in gold ink on parchment paper. Then roll the invitation into a scroll and seal it with gold wax. Tie it with gold cording and a miniature pair of golden wedding rings.
- Have a piece of wedding anniversary cake delivered in a gold-foil box tied with a gold-organza ribbon.
- Send the invitation with a tulle-wrapped bundle of gold-coated candied almonds, tied with a wide gold ribbon.
- Send a metallic-gold-colored wineglass containing the message "Come fill with golden anniversary fun."
- Send a small gold clock or timepiece with the note "You're invited to the golden anniversary hour."

- Send a small gold-painted pot filled with foil-wrapped chocolate coins and the note "We've found a golden love at the end of the rainbow. Please join us for a golden treasure celebration."
- Send a plastic golden egg along with a copy of *Jack and the Beanstalk*.

Special Instructions for Guests

Please bring a golden memory about the anniversary couple to share.

Decorating Touches

Cover the entire area with the golden touch of Midas. Decorate as simply or as elaborately as you wish using one or more of these ideas:

For the Room
- Drape the walls with swags of gold lamé cloth, placing decorative "50" numerals at the gathered peaks.
- Decorate a golden wedding haven to envelop the anniversary in romantic splendor, as described in this book's introduction.
- Float white and gold balloons to the ceiling with matching dangling ribbons. (Make sure the bottoms of the ribbons are well above guests' heads.)
- Place a gold-framed large black picture mat (velvet or satin wrapped) just beyond the party entrance. Fill this with a collage of wedding photos and memorabilia for golden reminiscing.
- Place white doves or lovebirds in a gilded cage as a lovely conversation piece.
- Line the room with metallic-gold or gold-painted artificial Christmas trees.
- Wrap the bar with one long strip of metallic-gold paper.
- Showcase a champagne fountain flowing with golden champagne.
- Drape sheer gold cloth over twinkle lights hanging from the ceiling.
- Hang gold wedding bells from the ceiling.

For the Table

- Make a lovely tablecloth statement using a gold-paint pen to write "I love you" along the edges of a white organza tablecloth.

- Make golden heart tablecloths and matching napkins. Dip a potato-cut stencil or rubber-stamp heart shape in gold paint to create stencil designs on sheer white fabric.

- Gather white organza tablecloths with tasseled gold cord tied with large attractive knots.

- Cover tables with gold lamé tablecloths or white tablecloths gathered with gold lamé bows. Complement the table ensemble with gold lamé chair covers or white chair cloths with gold lamé sashes.

- At the party entrance, present each guest with one of these unique table assignments, each printed with a table number. Once guests take the table assignment to their table, it will also serve as a decorative table accent and party favor. These items can also be prepositioned at individual place settings as place cards. In this case, attach a place card to the item or write the guest's name directly on the item.

  —Gold, ribbon-tied envelope marked "love letter"

  —Gold-sprayed red rose tied with a gold ribbon

  —Gold cupid ornament

  —Decorative gold mask

  —Plastic golden egg

  —Small, gold gift-wrapped box of candy such as Godiva chocolates

  —Gold garter

  —Small, gold bridal bouquet

  —Gold-laced corsage or boutonniere

  —Gold-printed table number on crisp white card stock (Attach tiny golden wedding bands to each card.)

  —Gold glass-ball Christmas ornament or a white one inscribed with gold ink

  —Gold-printed love poem (As a romantic option, search for a poem written from the groom to his bride.)

  —Gold-painted toy boat ("sailing on the sea of love")

  —Gold fan

  —Leaf inscribed with gold ink

—Bottle of wedding bubbles tied with a gold ribbon

—Tiny gold bell ringing with anniversary wishes. (Using thin gold ribbon, tie a note to each bell reading, "Ring to Inspire a Golden Wedding Kiss.")

—Gold English cracker (Purchase a commercial version or make one by wrapping cardboard tubes filled with sweets, mottoes, or small favors with ecru tissue paper. Tie the ends with a pretty gold ribbon, then roll and paste a gold doily around the tube.)

—Tie a piece of gold-painted or foiled fruit with a sheer piece of tulle or translucent ribbon. Attach a place card with the guest's name written in gold ink. (This looks great with the gold-fruit centerpiece described below.)

• Grace each place setting with these golden ideas:

—Trim napkins with gold cording, ribbon, or gold heart trinkets.

—Drape a swirl of gold bead garland or cord over a folded napkin.

—Wrap each napkin with a gold-sprayed leaf attached to a wire.

—Tie napkins with wide, sheer gold ribbons.

—Place a gold taper candle secured with florist's clay in a wineglass at each place setting. Fill the glass a third full with gold beads or marbles, then tie a gold ribbon around the rim.

—Fold a gold doily over a triangle-wrapped napkin topped with a flower bloom.

—Decoupage the back of glass plates with photos of the couple at their wedding. Arrange the photos over a layer of gold paper.

—Place each dinner plate over a stunning gold doily.

• Try one of these golden anniversary centerpiece creations. Place the centerpieces on reflective mirror tiles and sprinkle their bases with lustrous gold glitter and confetti:

—Wrap the base of gold candelabra with sheer white tulle.

—Wrap several white candle tapers together using gold, nonflammable ribbon or cording. (Hint: Do not burn the candles past the ribbon.) Secure this grouping in a crystal bowl with florist's clay. Conceal the clay with gold tree-ornament balls and randomly draped gold bead garlands.

—Place gold-painted or foiled fruit on a silver or crystal cake stand. Spray the fruit lightly, letting its true color show through in places, and trim with green ivy. Accent this centerpiece with the corresponding matching fruit place cards described above.

—Wrap champagne bottles with metallic gold gift-wrap and tie them with gold helium balloons.

—Place arrangements of gold photo frames, containing photos of the anniversary couple and their family, in the center of the table.

—Place gold-ball ornaments on an arrangement of crystal candlesticks.

—Make a gold-Mylar-balloon or gold-latex-balloon bouquet centerpiece. Weight it with either a gold gift bag or a sand-filled, paper-tied gold Mylar pouch.

—Wrap gold mesh around a gold or crystal vase and fill the vase with beautiful white flowers.

—Using florist's clay, attach a white gardenia, peony, or other large flower to the bottom of a clear globe or glass container filled with decorative gold stones. Gently pour water into the container and add a pair of swimming goldfish. Contact your local pet store to see if they might be willing to rent you the fish for a small fee, if you agree to place a small card by the centerpiece advertising their store. Otherwise, distribute centerpieces as door prizes.

—Float candles, gold confetti, and a white flower bloom in a crystal bowl filled with decorative gold stones.

—Use gold money trees as centerpieces.

—Encircle bowls of fruit with swirls of organza printed with gold stars. Spray fabric with star designs beforehand using paper-star templates.

—Fill gold baskets with flowers or plants. Lay a matching flower trimmed with a gold ribbon at each place setting.

—Set out gold, cocktail-sized table lamps next to white floral arrangements placed in gold containers.

—Display a single-layer wedding cake on each table. Place it on a raised gold cake stand or a crystal stand trimmed with gold ribbons.

Theme-Inspired Activities and Entertainment

Provide a gold-rush of excitement for this anniversary celebration. Choose one or more of the following golden moment activities.

- During a special golden anniversary moment, encourage guests to share a memory of the anniversary couple. Also, ask the anniversary couple to share their marriage and lifetime anecdotes. Record these recollections as a lasting memory. Videotaped recordings can be edited and complemented with the couple's favorite music. These moments can also be prerecorded on video or audiotape and combined with special appearances for a *This Is Your Life* presentation.

- Hire a musician to play a golden harp.

- Play soft recordings of the original wedding ceremony and reception music.

- Dance on a gold-dusted dance floor (use gold confetti) to an orchestra, DJ, or dance band playing music from the wedding year as well as the couple's favorite tunes including "their song."

- Mirror the original wedding ceremony by repeating vows, cutting a cake, and sharing a special toast.

- Place a fiftieth wedding anniversary announcement in your local newspaper. Although these announcements used to serve as an invitation to a small community affair, today's announcement is more of a congratulatory piece.

- Present the anniversary couple with a congratulatory note from the First Family. Upon request, a special card signed by the President will be sent to your loved one. You may also be able to obtain one from your state's governor. (See the *Supplier Resource Directory*.)

- Capture the golden moment with instant photos of the anniversary couple taken with each guest as an anniversary party favor.

- Show a special video made of short takes from the couple's home movie archives.

- Take a group photo to send with thank-you notes after the party.

- Direct a *Newlywed Game* skit, asking and matching answers of the anniversary couple.

- Present a "fashion throughout the marriage" show, showcasing fashion changes over the couple's married years. If possible, use actual clothing from their closet including their original wedding costumes.
- Give guests gold-ink pens to sign a wall mural with greetings and wishes. Take a photo of the mural before taking it down after the party.
- Frame a wedding photo of the couple with a white or ecru photo mat. Then have everyone at the party sign the wedding mat as a memento for the couple. You can have a framer add the glass later.

Menu Ideas

In addition to an elegant dinner menu, recreate the original wedding cake and place it on a gold-lamé-covered table topped with swaged ecru lace or chiffon. Gather the swag with elaborate gold bows and floral accents. Place gold netting and white tulle bundles of gold candied almonds or gold-foiled candies next to the cake. Individual gold boxes of groom's cake would also make a delightful touch. Custom dictates that those placing this cake under their pillow will dream of their loves. Still another golden table idea is placing Mexican wedding cookies or wedding-bell-shaped sugar cookies in gold ribbon-tied, clear corsage bags next to the cake.

Consider this "gold star" dinner menu:

- Exquisitely arranged hors d'oeuvres placed on the glass of a golden photo frame
- Duck à l'Orange
- Beef Wellington
- French-cut string beans with mushrooms
- Crisp romaine lettuce with strawberries, feta cheese, and champagne dressing
- Golden twice-baked potatoes
- Heart-shaped rolls
- Individual bottles of sparkling champagne
- Edible twenty-four-carat gold anniversary cake (Treat guests with the royal touch by serving a cake decorated with edible twenty-four-carat gold sheets. The anniversary couple will feel like a king and queen, and the guests will feel like they are eating a fortune with this ancient Roman custom.)

Party Favors with Flair

Present each guest with a golden souvenir.

- Ecru note cards tied with a lovely gold ribbon
- Small, gold, doily-wrapped wedding bouquet
- Candy bundles, cake boxes, or wedding cookies displayed at the cake table (See the *Menu Ideas* section above.)
- Small, gold, gift-wrapped box of candy such as Godiva chocolates
- Gold glass-ball ornament (Or choose a white one inscribed with gold ink.)
- Small gold jewelry or music box
- Any of the smaller items suggested in the *Decorating Touches* section
- Florist-delivered corsage or boutonniere (Have it delivered before, after, or during the party.)
- Instant photos mentioned in the *Theme-Inspired Activities and Entertainment* section

Golden Fifties Sock Hop

Fifty years brings to mind a fifties celebration—1950s, that is. Drive in to this popular fiftieth anniversary theme for a "bop 'til you drop" sock hop. This party will certainly be a solid gold hit with both young and old. You could also celebrate the fiftieth anniversary with an era party representing another hit parade year such as the year the couple was married. Or, ask guests to bring a picture of themselves wearing their previous-era wedding clothes. They could even wear the real thing, taking those dated pastel bridesmaids dresses and ruffled tuxedo shirts out of the mothballs.

For a 1950s celebration, ask guests to put on their poodle skirts and grab their letter sweaters. It's also fun to ask them to come dressed as a character from a 1950s song. Invite guests to this nostalgic party with an invitation trimmed with Bazooka bubble gum pieces. Or, include invitation details with a sock, a diary page, or a fifties 45 RPM record. Also, ask each guest to bring a vintage 45 to trade.

Hold this sock hop mixer in a high school gymnasium, real or created. Bring in lockers, basketball hoop, and bleacher facades or murals. Float pink, white, and black balloons near the ceiling with dangling ribbons.

Cover the walls with photos of fifties celebrity heartthrobs such as James Dean, Fabian, Sandra Dee, and Marilyn Monroe. Hang college pennants and fifties era fashions on the wall including leather jackets, poodle skirts, bowling shirts, letter sweaters, and rolled-up jeans.

Lay bubble-gum-pink tablecloths on the table and trim them with sock-hop socks. Top the tables with these fifties table accents: 33 RPM album-cover place mats, napkin rings made from sunglasses slipped over black napkins, Slinky toys as place cards, and saddle-shoe centerpiece arrangements. To make the saddle-shoes centerpiece, slide a drinking glass as a vase into a bobby sock and place one into each black-and-white saddle shoe. Fill the vases with fresh or silk pink carnations.

Another cute centerpiece is a floral ice cream soda arrangement. Fill a pink-painted soda glass with white carnations to form the soda "foam." Add a pair of straws and a miniature red carnation as the cherry topping. Place this arrangement on a vinyl record. Soda or banana split centerpieces can also be easily made by filling fountain containers with shiny glass Christmas bulbs and colorful curly ribbon accents. Another edible looking centerpiece can be made with a floral ice-cream-cone arrangement. Place a pink carnation flower "scoop" in ice cream cones and arrange these in a bowl with white daisies and fresh cherries, resembling a whipped cream topping.

Make vinyl-record potato chip and dip bowls. Melt a vinyl record over a metal bowl by heating it in the oven for a few minutes until it forms a bowl shape. (Do not let it melt completely and make sure the kitchen is well ventilated.)

Roll in a pink Cadillac convertible or a fast hot-rod roadster for cruisin' and lover's lane photo favors. Rent a jukebox or bring in a Wolfman-Jack-style DJ to spin golden oldies such as Pat Boone's "April Love" and Elvis Presley's "Love Me Tender." Play twisting and rocking tunes like "Rock around the Clock" and "Peppermint Twist" during various contests (sock hop dance, hula hoop, bubble blowing, and so on). Crown the anniversary prom king and queen and present their royal highnesses with gifts of gold splendor. Hire an Elvis look-alike entertainer to mingle with the crowd and sing a few songs. Create a drive-in movie screen by projecting an old James Dean movie or the musical *Grease* on the wall. Have pink-clad diner waitresses, wearing "Flo" and "Gerty" name tags and funky advertisement buttons, take anniversary blue-plate special orders. Offer this menu served on a blue paper plate: cheeseburger, French fries, and a cherry Coke or malt.

Soda jerk or carhop characters can also roll around on roller skates delivering trays of after-school snacks such as bite-sized pieces of Hostess Twinkies, Snowballs, Spam, and Velveeta. In addition, invite guests to pull up a stool at a soda fountain counter for old-fashioned sodas, banana splits, root beer floats, and sundaes.

Ropin' Fifty Anniversary

Round up the gang at the ol' family ranch to join Jack and Jane's "Ropin' the big 5-0" anniversary." It's going to be a "yippee-i-o" celebration. Send small rope lariats looped around gold number "50" invitations. Or, send gold-rope-tied miniature root beer mugs filled with a "Come fill me up at the party" message. Roy Rogers or old west note cards or post cards would also make good invitations.

Tie your horse to the hitching post outside and swing open saloon doors to a room filled with gold, "50"-marked balloons and "home-on-the-range" music. Decorate western ranch tables with flannel tablecloths designed with horses, branding-iron marks, or other cowboy images. Top tables with stand-up rope lariats painted gold and looped with wire around a "50." Tie brown napkins with a piece of rope glued with a gold nugget. Place a beer mug at each place setting. Write a different western hero or outlaw name with a gold paint pen on each mug (Roy Rogers, Annie Oakley, Billy the Kid, Jesse James, and so on). Hang a rope and gold-nugget-trimmed cowboy hat on the back of each ladder-back wooden chair, turned around to allow guests to sit horse-style.

Hang pictures of horses around the room. Accent the room with split rail fencing, hitching posts, wagon wheels, hay stacks, and horse saddles. Light a roaring fire in the stone fireplace, complete with a large banner hanging above it spelling out this message with rope: "Jack and Jane's Ropin' 50th Anniversary!" The couple can tie the knot for a second time in front of their family and friends.

Challenge the cowboys to an old-fashioned western shootout. Pass out squirt gun favors to shoot out taper-candle flames. Secure the candles (using florist's clay) to gold-painted aluminum pie tins nailed to the split rail fence. Follow this with a rootin' tootin' rodeo. Start with the golden-calf-ropin' event. Rope stick-horse toys attached to gold-painted sawhorses. Attach fur tails to the horses with a nail. Then blindfold guests for some more horsin' around, pin-the-"50"-tail-on-the-donkey fun.

Organize singing cowboys (family) to serenade guests while they load their plates in the buffet line. Win cowboys' hearts with western steak and baked potatoes served with oven-baked beans, mini corn-on-the cob, horseshoe-shaped biscuits, and tossed salad with western or ranch dressing. After dinner, pull up to the bar for root beer floats and "cowboy coffee" cake. Then clear the floor for an old-fashioned western square dance. Send guests home with gold bolo ties, gold rope barrettes and brooches, and long ropes of licorice.

Swashbuckling Pirate's Gold Bash

Invite guests to join the anniversary couple for a swashbuckling pirate's bash and gold treasure hunt. Send a gold-painted pirate's eye patch along with a crumpled treasure map leading to the anniversary party location, which is marked with an "X" and the word "gold." Roll the map into a corked bottle or put it in the mouth of a plastic crocodile.

Greet party mates with a Long John Silver character, complete with a parrot on his shoulder and a peg leg. He should invite guests to "walk the plank" under pirate flags and seagulls to the party area. Invite live alligators to walk around the party, reminding guests of the famous pirate from *Peter Pan*, Captain Hook. (See the *Supplier Resource Directory* for source.) Decorate the pirate hideout with a gold pirate ship's sail and gold-painted anchors, crates, and skull-and-crossbones markings. Have shifty-looking pirates clad in red-and-white-striped shirts and gold bandannas lead guests to their tables by holding fake pistols or swords to the "prisoners'" backs. Cover tables with jagged-edged, gold lamé tablecloths topped with a ship in a bottle or a treasure chest overflowing with gold coins. Illuminate either centerpiece with gold votive candles. Lay a pirate's hat over each guest's plate. Write guests' names on skull and crossbones props. (Purchase these from a costume shop or in the Halloween section of a retail store.)

Hand each guest a gold lobster mallet (paint the handles only) and gold bib for lobster bake fare. Add hush puppies, crab cakes, cole slaw, and clam chowder. Serve gold tankards of ale and golden punch. After dinner, lead guests on a treasure hunt to the couple's golden anniversary gifts and a treasure-chest-shaped anniversary cake. Send every guest home with gold booty (a bag of gold foil chocolate coins).

Anniversary Gift Suggestions

Choose one of these golden anniversary treasures:

- Gold memory box for photos and keepsakes
- Gold-engraved plate commemorating the occasion
- Matching gold watches
- Gold-framed family reunion photo (Take the photo at the anniversary party and present it later to the anniversary couple.)
- Fifty roses in a gold vase
- Fifty-dollar gift certificate or check, folded and placed in a gold photo frame
- Gold anniversary clock to be set on each wedding anniversary
- Tickets to a performance at the symphony, ballet, or theater
- Gold magnifying glass
- Matching "pure as gold" heart key chains
- Collection of golden oldie tunes
- Gold photo album
- Golden antique treasure such as a phonograph, old book, small table, or other prize antique
- Personalized golden treasure (Carefully consider an item the couple has always wanted or needed such as a couch, recliner chairs, new car, or bill or mortgage payoff. Pool resources with family and friends to present the couple with one large gift.)

A Special Moment for the Anniversary Couple

A Golden Trip down Memory Lane

Plan an anniversary trip down memory lane. Have a limousine driver follow a predetermined itinerary. Write tourist-guide information for each stop or record the details on a tape recorder, instructing the anniversary couple to play and turn off the recorder at specified times. Perhaps the first location will be where the couple met such as a local high school or ice cream parlor. Is the site long gone? Don't worry! Memories can bring the picture to mind. Give the couple envelopes containing clues to the next location such as a matchbook or ticket stub from a local restaurant or art museum where the couple used to date. In one envelope, insert a copy of their wedding invitation or wedding announcement hinting at the original wedding site where they can enjoy anniversary cake and champagne. (Note: Send the couple on a "just for two" journey or, if they prefer, arrange for close family members to join them.)

The Fifty-Fifth Anniversary
—Emerald—

Toast: A Traditional Irish Blessing - May the road rise up to meet you.
May the wind be always at your back.
May the sun shine warm upon your face,
And the rain fall soft upon your fields.
And until we meet again, may the Lord
Hold you in the hollow of his hand.

The "luck of the Irish" has certainly blessed a fifty-five year marriage. The anniversary couple is precious and rare as a sparkling emerald, the traditional anniversary designation symbolizing charity, understanding, and a noble spirit. This anniversary also has been observed as an Emerald Isle celebration, recognizing the beautiful land of Ireland. Celebrate this fifty-fifth anniversary with an emerald green celebration steeped in Irish lore. You don't have to be Irish to appreciate its lucky charm.

Emerald Isle Fantasy

Covered in emerald splendor, this Emerald Isle will pay tribute to a jeweled love. Create a magnificent Emerald Isle fantasy in honor of the anniversary couple.

Invitation Ideas

Send an emerald invitation gem to each guest.

- Photo-framed invitation trimmed in faux emerald
- Invitation printed with green ink and enclosed with a green-painted Blarney Stone (Kiss the Blarney Stone with red lipstick for good luck!)
- Hand-delivered invitation and shamrock plant
- Invitation details glued directly on a Lucky Charms cereal box
- Engraved invitation trimmed with emerald rhinestones
- Invitation that includes a shamrock and a lucky green penny

Special Instructions for Guests

Enclose a safety-pinned "green" dollar bill with this note: "There'll be a wear'n' o' the green for this special occasion. Please dress in green to celebrate the couple's emerald love."

Decorating Touches

Create a beautiful emerald green vision.

For the Room

- Float emerald green and white balloons with dangling ribbon tails from the ceiling.
- Hang Irish tapestries on the wall.
- Hang Irish travel posters on the wall such as the Cliffs of Moher or Blarney Castle.
- Cover one wall with a rainbow mural. At the end of the rainbow, place a "pot of gold" (a gold-painted washtub) on a decorated table to collect cards and gifts for the anniversary couple.

For the Tables

- Cover tables with floor-length, emerald green tablecloths topped with an Irish lace table runner or circle.
- Lay out fine Irish linen tablecloths.

- Add one of these emerald-fantasy centerpieces:
  —Belleek china teapots filled with shamrock plants
  —Waterford crystal bowl filled with a single floating gardenia, gold floating candles, and green metallic confetti
  —Gilded pot overflowing with gold coins and emeraldlike jewels
  —Place a lush green plant in a basket and accent the base of the plant with Irish potatoes. A leprechaun figurine would also add a delightful touch to the basket arrangement. Tie the basket with an emerald green satin bow.
- Choose one of these emerald place card holders for each place setting:
  —Leprechaun figurine
  —Raw potato (Write the guest's name with green paint directly on the potato.)
  —Emerald-rhinestone-trimmed place card
  —Small Bells of Ireland plant
  —Shamrock plant placed in a shamrock-design teacup
  —Miniature box of Lucky Charms cereal
  —Photo frame trimmed with faux emerald, containing a wedding picture of the anniversary couple
  —Blarney Stone painted green and kissed with red lipstick for good luck
- Include a "wee bit" of the Irish with each place setting:
  —Place an emerald green doily under each plate.
  —Use Irish Waterford crystal and Belleek china place settings.
  —Make a medieval statement by gluing emerald "jewels" to pewter plates and goblets.
  —Wrap an Irish linen napkin with an emerald-studded pewter napkin ring, a glittering shamrock napkin ring ornament, a Claddagh-design napkin ring, or a Celtic knotwork wedding-band-design napkin ring. A Tara brooch pinned to an emerald green velvet ribbon wrap would also make an elegant statement.
  —Hide a small card bearing an Irish blessing on each saucer and under each coffee cup. Here are two blessing ideas: "May good fortune be yours, and may your joys never end!" and "Long live the Irish, long live their cheer! Long live our friendship year after year!"

Theme-Inspired Activities and Entertainment

Spread Irish cheer with Emerald Isle fun.

- Play Celtic music as guests arrive.
- Stage a short bagpipe performance to announce the cake cutting and anniversary toast. (Hint: Bagpipes are very loud. Keep the performance short and stage this entertainment in a large room or outdoors.)
- Offer an Irish blessing for the anniversary couple before dinner.
- During dinner, arrange for a harpist or flutist to play romantic Irish tunes.
- Hire a tenor vocalist to entertain guests with classics like "Danny Boy" and to lead the group in an Irish song sing-along.
- Hire entertainers to perform a short Scottish folk dance or an Irish step dance, similar to a *Riverdance* performance.
- Conduct a green penny hunt for the children.
- Organize a "pinning o' the green" dollar dance. Guests pin a dollar bill on the anniversary couple, or hand a dollar to an attendant, to dance with the anniversary bride or groom.
- Invite guests to share a "tall Irish tale" memory of the anniversary couple.

Menu Ideas

Offer an Irish menu of Emerald Isle delights.

- Corned beef and cabbage
- A potato bar filled with a variety of potato treats. Include Irish baked potatoes with a choice of toppings such as cheese, bacon bits, salsa, chives, sour cream, and so on. Add an array of potato salads and potato dishes such as scalloped potatoes and ham, au gratin potatoes, Irish mashed potatoes (a potato and cabbage combo), home-fried potatoes, hash browns, French fries, twice-baked potatoes, potato pancakes, whipped potatoes and chives, creamed potatoes and peas, sweet potatoes, and Potatoes O'Brien (home-fried potatoes and green pepper).
- Pot-of-gold soup (Pour cheese soup into pot-shaped or pottery bowls.)
- Irish stew

- Emerald green vegetables such as peas and asparagus with lime juice
- Green pepper salad bowls filled with a dollop of salad dressing and fresh raw vegetables including carrot sticks, green onions, celery sticks, and radishes
- Green, shamrock-shaped fruit-medley Jell-O mold
- Irish coffee
- A wedding cake decorated with green sugar shamrocks
- Chocolate brownies topped with vanilla ice cream and green crème de menthe
- Green beer flowing freely from "O'Malley's Pub" (inscribe the name above the bar)

Party Favors with Flair

Thank each lad and lass for coming to the anniversary celebration with one of these at-the-end-of-the-rainbow treasures.

- Irish linen hankie
- Irish-design Christmas tree ornament
- Four-leaf clover or emeraldlike pendant, brooch, key chain, or tie tack
- Small Waterford crystal or Belleek china memento
- Small photo frame trimmed with faux emerald, with a wedding picture of the anniversary couple
- Pair of green Irish wool mittens or knit scarf
- Small leprechaun figurine
- Small Bells of Ireland plant
- Shamrock plant placed in a shamrock-design teacup

Green Eggs and Ham and Other Green Shenanigans

Here's a Dr. Seusslike prescription for a fun and fanciful emerald green celebration. Invite guests to share some storybook shenanigans in honor of the young-at-heart anniversary couple. Serve a "green eggs and ham" breakfast meal. Dr. Seuss has this to share on the art of eating green eggs and ham:

"I do not like green eggs and ham!
I do not like them,
Sam-I-am.
You do not like them.
So you say.
Try them! Try them!
And you may.
Try them and you may, I say."
—from *Green Eggs and Ham,* by Dr. Seuss

Make unique "green eggs and ham" table centerpieces to be awarded to the table's best shenanigan. Just before guests arrive, place a whole cooked ham on a platter. Wrap the ham first with aluminum foil and then with decorative green Mylar paper. Stick a large cooking fork into the top of the ham. Place this on a platter with two hard-boiled eggs dyed green. Stand a large copy of Dr. Seuss's *Green Eggs and Ham* on the platter. If you like, attach a stuffed, white-gloved "hand" to the edge of the book or to the top of the fork for a cartoonish look. Award the centerpiece to one of the guests during a "shenanigans" drawing. First, have each guest write a high-spirited or mischievous memory of the anniversary couple on a card. Collect the cards in a green hat placed at each table. One table member can then draw a card from the hat to determine the "Green Eggs and Ham" centerpiece winner. All the cards can then be taken to the head table for a random selection reading in front of all the guests.

Direct each guest to his or her table by placing a table number inside a copy of *Green Eggs and Ham*. Each guest will find his or her place setting marked by a green-dyed hard-boiled egg printed with the guest's name. Place an additional copy of *Green Eggs and Ham* on each table as a unique menu card. Paste anniversary breakfast specials inside the book, listing a variety of "green eggs and ham" selections including scrambled green eggs and ham, sunny-side up green eggs and ham, green eggs and ham and flapjacks, and so on. Have the wait staff offer both green and traditional selections (for the faint of heart). Also, have the staff dress in "Cat-in-the-Hat" garb including tall, red-and-white-striped stovepipe hats.

Before closing the book on this novel celebration, arrange for a family member or costumed Dr. Seuss character to read *Green Eggs and Ham.* Then present a toast to the couple with mimosas (champagne and orange juice).

Emerald City of Love

Each guest will arrive to find an arrow sign on the party lawn reading, "This way to the Emerald City—just follow the yellow brick road." Draw yellow bricks with yellow chalk or paint the walkway with yellow, water-based paint. You can also make the yellow brick road with yellow-brick-painted butcher-block paper or a yellow, plastic tablecloth roll path. (Tape both down securely to avoid the possibility of tripping.) Line the yellow brick road with poppies. Cover the front door with green paper studded with shining emerald jewels and a sign reading, "Emerald City."

At the door, have the Emerald City Guardian of the Gates greet guests with "We're off to see the Wizard" music playing in the background. Inside the "city," everything is green. Dress the wait staff in green and cover the windows with green cellophane. Float emerald green balloons with dangling ribbon tails from the ceiling. As in *The Wizard of Oz,* clothe the gatekeeper in green from head to toe and give his skin and beard a green tint. On a side table, he should have a green box containing skeleton keys to the city, designating table numbers for guest seating. With his new friends Dorothy, the Tin Man, the Scarecrow, and the Cowardly Lion, he can greet guests and pass out seating assignments.

Place a pair of green-tinted spectacles (sunglasses) at each place setting. Attach a note explaining that these green-tinted spectacles are necessary to protect the guest from the blinding Emerald City glare. The guests' names can also be added as another seating-assignment option. Cover each Land of Oz table with floor-length, emerald green lamé cloths. For the table's centerpiece, place a pair of ruby red slippers on a reflective mirror tile. Make each pair of the famous ruby red shoes by gluing red sequins and glitter over a pair of red shoes. Surround the centerpiece with glowing votive candles, scattered green Mylar confetti, and emerald jewels.

The Emerald City's most famous citizen—the Wizard of Oz—was known for granting wishes. Have guests write their "somewhere over the rainbow" wishes for the anniversary couple in a special Emerald Anniversary Guest Book. (Attach additional blank pages in a copy of

The Wizard of Oz.) Present this book to the couple with a champagne toast.

Anniversary Gift Suggestions

Present the couple with one of these special gifts to commemorate their long, loving marriage.

- Matching Irish wool sweaters.
- Emerald green wool lap blankets for cuddling up in front of the fire or TV
- Matching Irish wool caps, hats, knit scarves, or mittens
- Irish linen tablecloth and napkin set
- Set of Irish linen sheets
- Identical Claddagh rings (or Celtic knotwork wedding bands)
- Irish wall tapestry
- Set of Celtic music tapes or CDs
- Box filled with Ireland post cards and a plane ticket to the Emerald Isle
- Fifty-five dollar gift certificate, check, or fifty five dollar bills
- Emerald green candy dish
- Set of emerald green crystal

A Special Moment for the Anniversary Couple

An Irish Blessing

Arrange for your spiritual or religious leader to offer an Irish blessing or emerald anniversary wish for your marriage. Share this sacred moment with each other only or invite your immediate family to enjoy the experience. Share a toast of wine or "green" grape juice from a single cup.

The Sixtieth Anniversary and Beyond
—Diamond—

*Toast: To a love and marriage that sparkles
with the brilliance of diamonds!*

Love abounds with sparkling diamond elegance in this sixty-year anniversary celebration. Some lists also designate the tenth, thirtieth, and seventy-fifth anniversaries with diamonds. No matter what anniversary year, celebrate this gem of an anniversary with diamond-filled splendor.

It's not so unlikely anymore that a couple will celebrate a sixty-year anniversary. The number of centenarians is on the rise, thanks to healthier living and advanced technology. Despite a high divorce rate, the number of marriges reaching and passing the half-century mark is rising. The National Center for Health Statistics reports that since 1985, divorce rates have been stable or slowly declining. Research suggests that nearly half of contemporary marriages could survive until death. Post-fifty-year anniversary celebrations should increase as a wave of baby-boomer marriages approach their golden fiftieth and beyond.

A Diamond Cotillion

Host a dazzling anniversary creation—a Diamond Cotillion. This wedding anniversary beautifully honors the couple's priceless love.

Invitation Ideas

Create an invitation of sparkling splendor.

- Fill an invitation with diamond dust (sparkling confetti or glitter).
- Attach a single diamond rhinestone to the invitation.
- Roll the invitation into a scroll and tie it with a simple white ribbon. Then place this scroll into a plastic corked bottle along with diamond rhinestones and silver glitter.
- Deliver this elegant invitation in a diamond-rhinestone-studded jewelry box.
- Cover a dinner bell with diamond rhinestones and invite guests to "Ring in a Diamond Anniversary Celebration."
- Wrap an invitation with a white ribbon studded with diamond accents.
- Borrow a diamond idea from the *Diamonds Are Forever* or *Breakfast at Tiffany's* sections.

Special Instructions for Guests

Ask guests to bring a photo of their "diamonds in the rough" (children) to give to the anniversary couple. Provide a plastic sleeve with a label for photo identification.

Decorating Touches

Cover this diamond cotillion in dazzling elegance.

For the Room

- Scatter a "diamond dust" pathway into the party area using confetti and glitter. Scatter diamond rhinestones off to the sides to prevent people from slipping.

- Cover the ceiling with sparkling "diamonds" (strands of twinkle lights covered with sheer white fabric).
- Drape the bar in black velvet and attach diamond gems and rhinestones to it.
- Frame the orchestra's stage with dramatic sheer white curtains and hang elaborate ostrich-feather fans behind the orchestra, up-lighted with soft lights.
- Hang a large, elaborate frame backed with black velvet near the party entrance. Attach various photos of the couple throughout the years.
- Browse the *Diamonds Are Forever* and *Breakfast at Tiffany's* sections for décor suggestions.
- Place a diamond-studded guest book at the entrance for collecting guests' signatures.
- Make a sparkling room centerpiece. Drape the cake table in black velvet. Showcase a three- or four-tiered cake topped with a diamond rhinestone "60" (or other anniversary year) outline. Glue diamond rhinestones to the cake columns. Build the cake on a mirrored platform and scatter diamondlike gems at its base. A sparkling champagne fountain gracing each side of the cake table would also be spectacular.

For Tables

- Cover the head table with a bank of white flowers dusted with silver glitter.
- Overlay floor-length, white satin tablecloths with silver lace. Cover chairs with white satin covers and a silver sequin sash.
- Cover tables with floor-length, white cloths. Top with sheer white organza dotted with small rhinestone accents. Cover silver-cane chairs with sheer fabric and add fresh green garland accented with pale pink roses and a sheer bow studded with diamond accents.
- Choose from one of these diamond centerpiece creations:
  —Place a diamond-studded silver candelabrum as the table centerpiece, set with a beautiful white flower arrangement and white taper candles.
  —Fill diamond-studded vases with pale pink roses. Place each vase on a mirror tile and scatter diamond rhinestones at its base.

—Decorate with centerpiece vignettes of days gone by. Place a variety of antique bowler hats and elaborate ladies' hats on hat stands. Drape a jewelry box with vintage jewelry, pearls, and faux diamond treasures. Add long gloves, antique opera glasses, handled mirrors, brushes, or perfume bottles. Delicately accent these items with rhinestones. Add a vintage glove, perfume bottle, or Victorian calling card, all accented with rhinestones, at each place setting as a novel place card.

—Set each table with a cake surrounded by faux diamond jewelry.

• Shower the table with these place setting accents:

—As guests arrive, hand them a small diamond-studded heart frame with their names and table numbers.

—Wrap white napkins with strings of rhinestone gems.

—Set each place setting with a diamond-trimmed vase and a single rose tied with a small card bearing the guest's name in silver ink.

—Place a mirror tile under each guest's plate and sprinkle it with diamond rhinestones. Place a diamond-accented crystal votive candle at each place setting

—Glue faux diamond baubles on clear glass plates and goblets.

• Browse the *Diamonds Are Forever* and *Breakfast at Tiffany's* sections for décor suggestions.

Theme-Inspired Activities and Entertainment

A true cotillion once included an elaborate quadrille dance and a dance led by a couple at the ball. The formal ball was elaborately structured and rarely had theme decorations or trendy music. Today, we take thematic license granted by life-long love to create an elegant, modern interpretation of the traditional diamond anniversary celebration.

• Have an MC announce the anniversary couple with dazzling fanfare. Turn off the lights and use sparklers to welcome the couple. (Provide notice before turning off the lights to alert those who might be moving about. See *Supplier Resource Directory* for source.)

• Provide an orchestra for soft dinner music and ballroom dancing. Begin the first dance, led by the anniversary couple, by proposing a sparkling champagne toast to the couple.

- Present a diamond-studded photo album containing photos of the "diamonds in the rough" (children) of the couple's family and friends. If possible, have designated people assemble this album during dinner. If the collection is extensive, place a few photos in the album and explain that the gift will be completed after the party.
- Have the couple's children form a greeting line to welcome guests as they arrive. Make sure the photo display and greeting line are spaced appropriately apart to ensure a smooth crowd flow.
- Take instant photos of guests with the anniversary couple as a lasting memory. Glue a diamond rhinestone in the corner of each photo.

Menu Ideas

Serve a sparkling, twenty-four-carat, seated-dinner menu.
- Chicken à la Sparkle (roasted chicken breasts marinated in champagne and served with a side of apple, cinnamon, and raisin sauce)
- "Fourteen-carrot" honey-glazed baby carrots
- Fruit salads soaked in sparkling champagne and served in champagne goblets
- Wild rice pilaf
- Crystal bowls filled with a variety of dinner breads including dinner rolls, pumpernickel, rye, cinnamon rolls, and cheese bread sticks
- An ice cream dessert placed in a crystal ice bowl (See "The Fifteenth Anniversary: Crystal" chapter, page 106, for how-to directions.)
- Bottles of sparkling cider

Party Favors with Flair

Place dazzling cotillion mementos on each guest's plate or at the cake table.
- Faux diamond pendants, brooches, tie tacks, cuff links, or key chains placed in velvet jewelry gift boxes
- Diamond-studded photo frames or vases described above as place setting décor
- Diamond-studded instant photos of each guest with the anniversary couple

- A single pale pink rose tied with a silk ribbon adorned with a single diamond rhinestone
- A box of Cracker Jack containing a diamond ring prize (Insert a ring from a toy store or party favor supplier.)

Breakfast at Tiffany's

Like Holly Golightly said in *Breakfast at Tiffany's,* "You'll be crazy about Tiffany's." Remember, Holly "didn't give a hoot" about jewelry —"except diamonds, that is." This posh celebration of fabulous fakes can be held as a late morning brunch, the perfect daytime celebration for the older anniversary couple. It also makes an exciting after-theater, midnight breakfast for the jet-set sixty-year anniversary crowd. After business hours, you might even be able to rent a jewelry store for this "Breakfast at Tiffany's" party. Of course, the owner may request that the store be heavily guarded, which will enhance the department store atmosphere.

You could also throw the party at home. Hang an "Open" sign listing "store hours" on the front door or window. Inside, create a jewelry store atmosphere with showcases and store-front window displays of "diamond" jewelry, a cash register, and suited salespeople. Hang crystal chandeliers from the ceiling. Place white-satin-draped tables among the display cases. Top each table with a million-dollar centerpiece. Drape a black velvet cloth over a shoebox for height. Then place "diamond" tiaras, necklaces, brooches, hat ornaments, and shoe buckles on the display. Wrap black napkins with diamond bracelets as napkin rings. Or, tie a white napkin with a long black glove and pin it with a diamond brooch. A diamond bracelet napkin ring and Audrey Hepburn-style sunglasses wrapped around a white napkin also look very chic. Place a faux diamond ring, diamond brooch, or diamond key chain (representing the key Holly Golightly was always without in the movie) in a velvet jewelry box (the kind where the lid springs up) as a unique place card holder. Like Holly says, "You can always tell what kind of a person a man thinks you are by the earrings he gives you." Set the table with fine china and cut-crystal glassware. Place a crystal ashtray filled with candy cigarettes at each table, too.

Invite guests by having a Danish and hot coffee delivered with the invitation. Holly's trademark cigarette holder would also make a cool invitation statement. Fill the party with genteel gossip, "Moon River" music, and first-time experiences. In the movie, Holly treats Paul to a "When was the last time you did something for the first time?" outing. Invite anniversary guests to do the same. Drink champagne before breakfast. Have your photo taken "casing a dime store." Put on a lampshade hat or a Halloween cat or dog mask for this movie photo moment. Send guests home with a "Tiffany's" shopping bag filled with a jewelry box containing a diamond costume jewelry piece, a Danish wrapped for the next morning, and a Cracker Jack box filled with a specially placed diamond ring toy.

If guests stay long after breakfast, send out for "reinforcements," as Holly Golightly would put it (party food and libations).

Diamonds Are Forever!

For this diamond-studded event, ask guests to "Wear diamonds, of course, darling!" White tuxedo dinner jackets and cocktail dresses are also recommended. Title this anniversary party "Diamonds Are Forever" in honor of the long-shared love between the anniversary couple. Prepare for a thrilling diamond adventure in this "Bond—James Bond" celebration. Send a diamond-studded toy revolver as a smoking invitation. Put this 007 party "undercover" with a black and silver color scheme to enhance the danger and intrigue lurking everywhere.

Float black and silver balloons with silver and black ribbon tails from the ceiling. Flash James Bond movies on one wall with the volume turned down. Cover tables with black, floor-length cloths. Top them with metallic silver or silver-sequined material. Make debonair James Bond-style napkins by wrapping crisp white napkins with black bow ties. Attach dice, diamond-suited playing cards, or casino chips to place cards. Shower diamond rhinestones over these singular place cards. Alternate tables with different 007 centerpieces including a large brandy snifter filled with diamonds, a diamond-studded pistol laid on a stack of Ian Fleming's James Bond books, or an attaché case filled with diamonds, a passport, and a clock bomb prop. Set a novel place card, a name-inscribed martini glass filled with green olives, at each place setting.

Serve martinis "shaken, not stirred" with a large slice of lemon peel in champagne goblets. Sneak an international spy message to the anniversary couple—hidden and baked inside the cake—on a silver medallion that reads "Y-R-A-S-R-E-V-I-N-N-A-D-N-O-M-A-I-D-Y-P-P-A-H" ("Happy Diamond Anniversary" spelled backward).

Anniversary Gift Suggestions

Diamonds are a girl's best friend, especially the diamond engagement ring. Perhaps the couple never could buy a diamond engagement ring, so surprise them with a stunning one. Or, present the couple with one of these diamond anniversary gifts.

- Matching diamond watches
- Faux diamond-trimmed photo frame
- Faux diamond-trimmed clock
- Diamond-cut crystal chandelier
- Check or gift certificate for sixty dollars (or more, depending on the anniversary number)
- Baseball-diamond coffee table book and tickets to a major or minor league baseball game
- Photo album studded with a faux diamond heart and filled with photos of the couple and their family throughout the years (See *Supplier Resource Directory* for source.)
- Diamond-headed cane
- Diamond- or rhinestone-trimmed dinner bell

A Special Moment for the Anniversary Couple

Diamond Lights Horse and Carriage Ride

Take a horse and carriage ride, just the two of you, under the diamond lights of the sky or city.

Appendix A

Wedding Anniversary Gifts

Anniversary	*Traditional*	*Modern*
First	Paper	Clocks
Second	Cotton	China
Third	Leather	Crystal or Glass
Fourth	Fruit or Flowers	Appliances
Fifth	Wood	Silverware
Sixth	Candy or Iron	Wood
Seventh	Wool or Copper	Desk Sets
Eighth	Bronze or Pottery	Linens or Lace
Ninth	Pottery or Willow	Leather
Tenth	Tin or Aluminum	Diamond Jewelry
Eleventh	Steel	Fashion Jewelry
Twelfth	Silk or Linen	Pearls
Thirteenth	Lace	Textiles or Furs
Fourteenth	Ivory	Gold Jewelry
Fifteenth	Crystal	Watches
Twentieth	China	Platinum
Twenty-fifth	Silver	Silver
Thirtieth	Pearl	Diamond
Thirty-fifth	Coral	Jade
Fortieth	Ruby	Ruby
Forty-fifth	Sapphire	Sapphire
Fiftieth	Gold	Gold
Fifty-fifth	Emerald	Emerald
Sixtieth	Diamond	Diamond

Source: 1998 Hallmark Cards, Inc.

Appendix B

Supplier Resource Directory

Most supplies for the decorations and activities described in this book can be found at party supply stores, craft supply stores, stationery or gift stores, import stores, department stores, discount stores, specialty stores, and other retail shops. International and specialty gifts are also sold in certain tea shops and restaurants. Some service businesses offer rental and purchase options and even carry party supplies. Check out your local rental stores (sometimes listed as party rental stores), costume shops, bridal fashion and formalwear shops, florists, and bakeries.

More and more party and decorating supplies are reaching the general consumer through common retail markets. However, you may wish to consult a party/event planner or decorating company for decorating and/or party planning services. Some cities are lucky enough to have theatrical suppliers or access to theatrical supply rentals from local theater or ballet groups, college theater departments, or high school drama departments. Find them in the Yellow Pages or other advertisement sources. Keep in mind that it may be possible to borrow from a friend or to find a great bargain at a local thrift shop, flea market, tag sale, or garage sale. Antique shops and Grandma's attic often have hidden party treasures. Also, use your imagination. If you can't find gold top hats, how about spraying the black top hats you found with gold spray paint? You can even make your own from thin cardboard. Can't find an animal-print tablecloth? Buy some novelty fabric from your local fabric shop and make your own. You can take the time to cut and hem each tablecloth, or you can simply cut the material edges with pinking sheers.

The Internet is a nearly inexhaustible source for party supplies and hard-to-find items. Also, numerous mail-order catalogs cater to a wide variety of specialty markets. These catalogs offer you the perfect theme-party accents right at your fingertips. I have collected a treasure trove of such suppliers and vendors and share them with you here.

Some one-of-a-kind items are hard to find unless you consult the resource directory below. As items become more popular, they naturally appear on your retailer's shelf. So, for ease and convenience, contact your local retail stores first to see if they carry the product. If you are unable to find it, call the manufacturer for the location of a retailer near you. As many sources require quantity or wholesaler purchases, you may want to see if your local retailer, party planner, or service vendor may be willing to special order the product for you.

Note: All the information below was researched and verified prior to publication, but some addresses and phone numbers may have changed in the meantime. The Internet is a constantly evolving reference source—website addresses change often. Also, the retail industry is volatile. New companies and innovative products appear and disappear at a high rate.

Theme-Oriented Decor and Clothing

Anderson's

Address: P.O. Box 1151, Minneapolis, MN 55440
Phone: (800) 328-9640

This company has various catalogs of theme-related centerpiece kits, party favors, and costume accessories. They specialize in supplying all-you-need kits and accessories for decorating school proms. However, their long list of themes, including *Titanic* and Middle Eastern themes, is the perfect source for theme-oriented anniversary parties. Assembly is required for kits.

Confederate Yankee

Address: P.O. Box 192, Guilford, CT 06437-0192
Phone: (203) 453-9900

You'll find Civil War era tin cup reproductions here that are perfect for "The Tenth Anniversary: Tin" party designs.

Decorative Novelty

Address: #74 - 20th Street, Brooklyn, NY 11232
Phone: (718) 965-8600, (800) 526-3668

This company sells decorative Mylar curtains, vinyl icicle props, metallic Christmas trees, and giant golden wedding bells. Their major market is retailers, but they are also willing to sell to the general public.

Gotcha Covered Linen Rentals

Address: 3815 Hessmer Avenue, Metairie, LA 70002-3211

Phone: (800) 426-1380

Rent specialty linens perfect for various anniversary themes, especially the lace, metallic, and novelty-theme designs. The "Roman classical" and "under the sea" chair covers are fantastic. This company prefers to rent to businesses, so ask your party site, party planner, or party rental company to order for you.

Sat'n Spurs Western Wear, Inc.

Address: 6452 E. Hampden Ave., Denver, CO 80222

Phone: (303) 757-7787

Website: www.satnspurs.com

This western boutique specializes in wedding costumes, accessories, and supplies that are perfect for western anniversary themes. You can find western design cake tops, invitations, garters, and more. Visit their website.

Senti-Metal

Address: 13701 E. 104th Ave., Commerce City, CO 80022

Phone: (303) 286-0111

If you can't find a bronzing service near you, try contacting this Colorado mom and pop service. They can electroplate a finish (bronze, gold, silver, and so on) on just about any item with a full lifetime warranty.

Sheplers

Address: P.O. Box 7702, Wichita, KS 67277

Phone: (800) 833-7007

This company claims to be "the world's largest western store and catalog." Call or write for a catalog of western clothes and products.

Sparktacular

Address: 5460 State Road 84, Bay 12, Fort Lauderdale, FL 33314

Phone: (877) 792-1101, (954) 792-1101

Website: www.sparktacular.com

Add a crowning touch to the anniversary celebration with Glitz super centerpiece sparklers. At a special moment, the sparklers go off to create forty-five seconds of sheer excitement. Contact this company to find a resource near you.

Specialty Catalogs

Expressions

Address: 120 North Meadows Road, Medfield, MA 02052
Phone: (800) 388-2699

This catalog has many unique gifts. Its inventory changes quite often, but it always has some cool items that complement theme parties perfectly. Currently, it is carrying a cute bear skin rug, flowerpot bread, and a wedding anniversary memory book that would fit in nicely with several of the anniversary themes.

Harriet Carter

Address: North Wales, PA 19455
Phone: (800) 377-7878, (215) 361-5122

This novelty and gift catalog has carried items such as a blue heart necklace (that replicates the beauty of the *Titanic* heart necklace) and gelatin molds that are perfect for making jewel anniversary salads.

Just Between Us

Address: 41 West 8th Ave, Osh Kosh, WI 54906
Phone: (800) 258-3750

This catalog carries a variety of gifts including a photo-tile-covered cherry box and a laser-photo wooden box that would make wonderful fifth-anniversary wooden gifts or favors. They also offer several first-anniversary invitation and favor ideas such as a photo paper doll and note pad cube. You could also have the couple's wedding photo printed on a cotton canvas pillow for a second-anniversary decoration or gift.

The Lighter Side Co.

Address: 4514 19th Street Court East, Bradenton, FL 34206-5600
Phone: (800) 244-9116

You'll find *Titanic* memorabilia and accents along with a voodoo doll, a self-playing electric violin, and other exciting items. Their inventory changes quickly, too.

Lillian Vernon

Address: Virginia Beach, VA 23479-0002
Phone: (800) 505-2250

This catalog carries thousands of gift items, many theme-related. One example is the red velveteen photo album decorated with a golden metal heart, studded with diamonds. Although their products change with the seasons, you'll be able to fine some great theme ideas for décor, invitations, and favors.

M&N International

Address: P.O. Box 64784, St. Paul, MN 55164-0784
Phone: (800) 479-2043

It's all here—wall decorations, theme cutouts, murals, ice molds, costume accessories, party decorations, and more.

The Mind's Eye, Memory Lane

Address: P.O. Box 6547, Chelmsford, MA 01824-0947
Phone: (800) 949-3333

This specialty catalog offers recordings of television commercials, TV hits, and so on. You can also find vintage French 1920s-style phones, brass candelabra, and classy hotel desk bells as well as original 1940s phones, tie-dye kits, Maltese Falcon statues, train whistles, and so on.

Oriental Trading Company, Inc.

Address: P.O. Box 3407, Omaha, NE 68103-0407
Phone: (800) 228-0122

This catalog is full of party favors, gifts, and party supplies covering many party themes. They have giant clown glasses, carnival game supplies, plush animals, thousands of small trinket favors, and much more.

Personal Creations Presented by Spiegel

Address: 142 Tower Dr., Burr Ridge, IL 60521
Phone: (800) 326-6626

You can find personalized gifts that could be used as anniversary party invitations, favors, or gifts. These high-quality gifts include custom wine bags, private-label champagne bottles, and six-inch fortune cookies containing personalized messages.

Past Times

Address: North American Office, Suite 400, 100 Cummings Center,
Beverly, MA 01915-6102
Phone: (800) 621-6020

This catalog carries fine gifts from Great Britain including beautiful tapestries, a Roman border ewer (pitcher) and fruit bowl, Celtic jewelry and music, and Victorian gifts.

Toscano

Address: 17 East Campbell Street, Arlington Heights, IL 60005
Phone: (800) 525-1233

This catalog of historical European reproductions for the home or garden will probably have that very-hard-to-find item. You'll see iron wall sconces, Roman sculptures and wall friezes, walking sticks, and a ship in a bottle. They also sell disguised leather book boxes and globe-covered anniversary clocks. Although pricey, they even carry an authentic red-colored British phone booth.

Wireless, Minnesota Public Radio

Address: P.O. Box 64422, St. Paul, MN 55164-0422
Phone: (800) 669-9999

This catalog offers nostalgic gifts for fans and friends of public radio. It is an excellent source for recordings of master composers, Celtic music, Broadway's best, and other music and gifts. They also have anniversary-perfect party supplies such as a chestnut roasting pan and a fir tree initial wreath.

Unique Invitations and Favors

The Adventure Group, Inc.

Address: 4720 Yender Ave., Lisle, IL 60532
Phone: (630) 960-5400

These folks sell numerous unique containers perfect for novel invitations. Examples include corked bottles, fire crackers, coconuts, video cases, film cases, mini tin trash cans, and more. Call to find a distributor near you. Let the distributor know you're interested in ordering in quantity or contact your local party rental store, party store, or party planner to see if they would be willing to place a special order for you.

America Goes Crackers, Inc.

Address: 656 North U.S. Hwy. #1, Pequesta, FL 33469
Phone: (800) 897-1822, (561) 745-5551

This company offers traditional British party crackers (small tubes filled with favors) in an endless array of theme designs. They can also create custom designs and fill party crackers with theme-related items.

Cookies by Design

Address: MGW Group, 1865 Summit Ave Suite 605, Plano, TX 75074
Phone: (800) 945-2665

These custom theme cookie bouquets are perfect for invitations, favors, centerpieces, and so on. They taste good, too! Call for a location near you.

The Crystal Cave

Address: 1141 Central Ave., Wilmette, IL 60091
Phone: (847) 251-1160

This company has a variety of crystal designs including a crystal cave, crystal rose, crystal clocks, crystal hearts, etched cityscapes, and other customized crystal gifts. These pieces would make spectacular invitations, favors, gifts, or centerpieces.

Fancy Fortune Cookies

Address: 6265 Coffman Rd., Indianapolis, IN 46268
Phone: (888) 776-6611, (317) 299-8900
Website: www.fortunecookiesonline.com

This company offers twelve flavors and colors of fortune cookies that you can personalize for your event. It also makes giant fortune cookies the size of a fist!

First Family Greetings

Address: Greetings Office, Room 39, The White House, Washington, DC 20500

Upon request, the President will send fiftieth and beyond anniversary greetings to the honored couple. The White House must receive the request four to six weeks prior to the occasion. They will need the recipients' full names (including Mr. and Mrs.), the address, the specific occasion (such as the fiftieth wedding anniversary or fifty-second wedding anniversary), and the date of the occasion.

First Impressions

Address: P.O. Box 581757, Minneapolis, MN 55458
Phone: (612) 424-9508

These folks make unique invitations or favors in an assortment of custom containers. They have silver serving tray invitations, corked bottles, booklike containers, firecracker-like containers, and more. They usually serve the wholesale market, so they do have large minimums. However, if you're throwing a big party, this may be a wonderful resource. Also, contact your local party rental store, party retailer, or party planner to see if they could place an order for you. They might also be willing to buy any extra pieces.

Nelson Trading Company

Address: 1230 Laurelwood Trail, Cummings, GA 30041
Phone: (800) 699-1859

This company sells live tree-seedling favors personalized with the anniversary couple's information.

Photonaps, BBJ Boutique Linens

Address: 7855 Gross Point Road, Skokie, IL, 60077
Phone: (800) 722-0126

These cloth napkins can be made with a photo design of the anniversary couple.

The Rose Lady

Address: P.O. Box 251, Los Alamitos, CA 90720
Phone: (888) 767-3523
E-mail: goldrose@msn.com
Website: www.theroselady.com

Order twenty-four carat gold collectibles perfect for the fiftieth anniversary celebration. You could purchase items such as a rose covered in twenty-four carat gold, gold-plated romantic cherubs, and an authentic gold-covered cigar.

The Safety Blaster, Corp.

Address: 6532 South Lavergne Ave, Bedford Park, IL 60638
Phone: (708) 496-8585

Make your next party a blast with this company's confetti-blaster party horns. These are great for nautical themes. Salute the anniversary couple with this unique item.

Wine Design

Address: 4901 Morena Blvd Suite 307, San Diego, CA 92017
Phone: (800) 201-9463, (858) 273-5695

This company sells exquisitely decorated private-label champagne and wines. Wine or champagne labels can be customized for your anniversary party. They also offer nonalcoholic beverages and special bottles containing candy.

Cakes and Edible Accents

Bridallink

Address: 5012 Mountain Lakes Blvd., Redding, CA 96003
Phone: (800) 725-6763
Web Site: www.wednet.com

Order a pack of six silver-plated wedding charms to bake in an anniversary cake or to use for a traditional Victorian cake pull. Each charm is attached to a white pulling ribbon and signifies a fortune. For example, the anchor charm brings hope and adventure, and the clover charm brings a "lucky in life" message.

Chocolates Ala Carte

Address: 13190 Telfair Avenue, Sylmar, CA 91342
Phone: (818) 364-6777, (800) 966-7440

This company creates chocolate mold sensations. They have a coffee cup and saucer mold perfect for the Fiesta Anniversary theme, plus chocolate pianos, chocolate elephants, chocolate Oscar statues, and many other cool thematic designs.

Elegant Catering

Address: P.O. Box 7003, Denver, CO 80207
Phone: (303) 367-0344

This catering company's signature is their royal line of twenty-four-carat-gold-decorated cakes. They offer services to supply you with the same twenty-four-carat yellow gold or white gold foiling that was used by early civilizations in food prepared for kings and queens. Treat your guests with this royal touch. They'll feel like they're eating a fortune.

Mike's Amazing Cakes

Address: 14934 N.E. 31st Circle, Redmond, WA 98052
Phone: (425) 869-2992

"You won't believe it's a cake!" Unusual, show-stopping 3-D cakes with unbelievable detail including a castle, guitar, oyster and pearl, pot of gold, movie theatre, and so on. Call for a brochure. They can ship just about anywhere. Open by appointment only.

Entertainment and Other Activities

Bwana Jim—Have Alligator Will Travel

Address: 2284 Deerwood Acre Drive, St. Augustine, FL 32086
Phone: (904) 824-4637 or (814) 697-7781

Bwana Jim will bring alligators and snakes to your theme anniversary party. This unique entertainment will certainly put some "bite" in your event!

Great Pumpkin Carriages, Inc.

Address: 926 N. Topeka Ave., Topeka, KS 66608
Phone: (800) 279-0897, (913) 233-2222

This company can ship a pumpkin carriage to transport the storybook anniversary couple. Although pricey, it'll make a lasting memory.

Song Sendsations, Custom Songs for Special Occasions

Address: Patty Sachs' Celebration Creations, 1172 Aston Cr., Burnsville, MN 55337

Phone: (612) 943-2420

This company will write a song parody using personal information as a surprise or a rousing sing-along tribute to the anniversary couple. They'll include a professionally recorded audio cassette along with a framed song sheet.

Publications to Help with Theme Accents

The "Party" Chest Newsletter

Address: Clear Creek Publishing, P.O. Box 102324, Denver, CO, 80250

Phone: (303) 671-8253

E-mail: raksparkle@aol.com

Keep up-to-date with the latest party ideas. The "Party" Chest is packed full of new party-planning ideas, supplier and service resources, and industry news. Subscriptions include a new theme design with every issue as well as a theme-design catalogue. Write or call for a free sample copy.

Party Creations *Book of Theme Event Design*

Address: Clear Creek Publishing-AB, P.O. Box 102324, Denver, CO, 80250

Phone: (303) 671-8253

E-mail: raksparkle@aol.com

Professional and novice planners worldwide have purchased this creative guide to unique and traditional theme events with creative flair. The guide includes sixty-seven complete, preplanned theme designs as well as a myriad of innovative ideas for creating your own. It contains planning tips and forms, unique invitations, enchanting table décor, party game mixers, fun and festive activities, and easy—yet elegant—party recipes.

Pick a Party *by Patty Sachs*

Address: Meadowbrook Press, 5451 Smetana Drive, Minnetonka, MN
55343
Phone: (800) 338-2232
Website: www.meadowbrookpress.com

Here's the new "bible" for party planners. Party expert Patty Sachs has included 160 party themes—more than any other book—to help readers turn holidays, birthdays, showers, and an evening with friends or family into special occasions. Call toll-free or visit our website to order.

Storybook Weddings *by Robin Kring*

Address: Meadowbrook Press, 5451 Smetana Drive, Minnetonka, MN
55343
Phone: (800) 338-2232
Website: www.meadowbrookpress.com

Here are fifty wedding themes to help a bride and groom create a unique event that will be remembered well past the couple's golden anniversary. Included are creative, theme-appropriate ideas for invitations; fashions and costumes for the entire wedding party; decor and special touches for the ceremony and reception; and entertainment and menu concepts. Call toll-free or visit our website to order.

Miscellaneous Resources

The Harry Fox Agency, Inc., A Subsidiary of National Music Publisher's Association, Inc.
Address: 711 Third Avenue, NY 10017
Phone: (212) 370-5330

Contact this agency for forms and license information. A license is required when copying recorded music to make unique cassette invitations. It's easy and inexpensive.

The Complete Wedding Planner

by Edith Gilbert

In this comprehensive guide, you'll find authoritative information on every aspect of a wedding, from the engagement to the honeymoon. It offers sensible, practical, up-to-date guidance on selecting rings, planning a rehearsal, wording invitations and announcements, managing a budget, selecting wedding attire, organizing a reception, choosing attendants, coping with florists, musicians, and photographers, and much more.

Order #6005

Storybook Weddings

by Robin Kring

Here are 50 wedding themes to help a bride and groom create a unique event that will be remembered well past the couple's golden anniversary. Included are creative, theme-appropriate ideas for invitations; fashions and costumes for the bride, groom, and the entire wedding party; decor suggestions for the ceremony and reception; and entertain-ment and menu concepts. Each special theme is designed to make for an unforgettable occasion.

Order #6010

The Joy of Marriage

by Monica and Bill Dodds

Here is a book of romance and love for married couples. With clever one-line messages, it accentuates the romantic, caring, and playful elements of married life. Filled with beautiful, touching black-and-white photographs, it's the perfect gift for weddings and anniversaries.

Order #3504

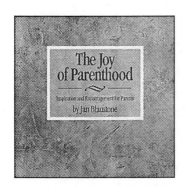

The Joy of Parenthood

by Jan Blaustone

Here is a treasury of warm advice and encouragement for that new parent in your life. This collection reflects the wittiest and wisest (and sometimes most amusing) sentiments ever written about raising families. Illustrated with 24 poignant photographs, it's the perfect gift to show a new parent your support.

Order #3500

The Dinner Party Cookbook

by Karen Brown

Here is a cookbook that makes enter-taining easy, with menus for 21 special-occasion and ethnic dinner themes. Includes 100 recipes and dozens of ideas for invitations, decorations, table settings, music, beverages, complete menus, and easy-to-follow recipes.

Order #6035

The Best Party Book

by Penny Warner

This book provides over 1,000 creative ideas for fun adult parties: anniversaries, birthdays, holidays, family and school reunions, bon voyages, baby showers, wedding showers, plus Super Bowl and Academy Awards parties.

Order #6089

Look for Meadowbrook Press books where you buy books. You may also order books by using the form printed below.

Order Form

Qty.	Title	Author	Order #	Unit Cost (U.S. $)	Total
	Best Party Book	Warner, P.	6089	$9.00	
	Best Baby Shower Book	Cooke, C.	1239	$7.00	
	Best Baby Shower Party Games #1	Cooke, C.	6063	$3.95	
	Best Bachelorette Party Games	Cooke, C.	6071	$3.95	
	Best Bridal Shower Party Games #1	Cooke, C.	6060	$3.95	
	Best Wedding Shower Book	Cooke, C.	6059	$7.00	
	Complete Wedding Planner	Gilbert, E.	6005	$15.00	
	Dinner Party Cookbook	Brown, K.	6035	$9.00	
	Familiarity Breeds Children	Lansky, B.	4015	$7.00	
	For Better And For Worse	Lansky, B.	4000	$7.00	
	Games People Play	Warner, P.	6093	$8.00	
	Happy Anniversary!	Kring, R.	6041	$9.00	
	Joy of Grandparenting	Sherins/Holleman	3502	$7.00	
	Joy of Marriage	Dodds, M. & B.	3504	$7.00	
	Joy of Parenthood	Blaustone, J.	3500	$7.00	
	Lovesick	Lansky, B.	4045	$7.00	
	Pick A Party	Sachs, P.	6085	$9.00	
	Pick-A-Party Cookbook	Sachs, P.	6086	$11.00	
	Something Old, Something New	Long, B.	6011	$9.95	
	Storybook Weddings	Kring, R.	6010	$8.00	
				Subtotal	
			Shipping and Handling (see below)		
			MN residents add 6.5% sales tax		
				Total	

YES! Please send me the books indicated above. Add $2.00 shipping and handling for the first book with a retail price up to $9.99 or $3.00 for the first book with a retail price over $9.99. Add $1.00 shipping and handling for each additional book. All orders must be prepaid. Most orders are shipped within two days by U.S. Mail (7–9 delivery days). Rush shipping is available for an extra charge. Overseas postage will be billed. **Quantity discounts available upon request.**

Send book(s) to:

Name _____ Address_____

City _____ State _____ Zip _____ Telephone (_____)_____

Payment via:

❑ Check or money order payable to Meadowbrook Press

❑ Visa (for orders over $10.00 only) ❑ MasterCard (for orders over $10.00 only)

Account # _____ Signature _____ Exp. Date _____

You can also phone or fax us with a credit card order.

A *FREE* Meadowbrook Press catalog is available upon request.

Mail to: Meadowbrook Press
5451 Smetana Drive
Minnetonka, MN 55343

Phone 612-930-1100   Toll-Free 800-338-2232   Fax 612-930-1940

For more information (and fun) visit our website:
www.meadowbrookpress.com

The Best Baby Shower Book

by Courtney Cooke

Here is a contemporary guide for planning baby showers packed with helpful hints, delicious recipes, checklists, designs for invitations and name tags, decorating ideas, a "wish list" for the mother-to-be, and engaging party games that are fun without being juvenile.

Order #1239

The Best Wedding Shower Book

by Courtney Cooke

This guide helps make wedding showers fun. It includes dozens of delicious recipes and menu ideas, imaginitive shower themes, gift suggestions, decorating ideas that don't cost a bundle, creative ideas for "couples' showers," practical party-planning checklists, and fun party games that won't embarrass your guests.

Order #6059